The Cultural Context
of Medieval Music

The Cultural Context
of Medieval Music

Nancy van Deusen

 PRAEGER

AN IMPRINT OF ABC-CLIO, LLC
Santa Barbara, California • Denver, Colorado • Oxford, England

Library of Congress Cataloging-in-Publication Data

Van Deusen, Nancy (Nancy Elizabeth)
   The cultural context of medieval music / Nancy van Deusen.
      p. cm.
   Includes bibliographical references and index.
   ISBN 978-0-275-99412-9 (hardcopy : alk. paper) —
ISBN 978-1-57356-996-5 (ebook)   1. Music—500-1400—
History and criticism.   2. Europe—Social conditions—To 1492.
I. Title.
   ML172.V78   2011
   780.9'02—dc23   2011030649

ISBN: 978-0-275-99412-9
EISBN: 978-1-57356-996-5

15   14   13   3   4   5

This book is also available on the World Wide Web as an eBook.
Visit www.abc-clio.com for details.

Praeger
An Imprint of ABC-CLIO, LLC

ABC-CLIO, LLC
130 Cremona Drive, P.O. Box 1911
Santa Barbara, California 93116-1911

This book is printed on acid-free paper ∞

Manufactured in the United States of America

Contents

List of Illustrations

Acknowledgements

Portions of these chapters have appeared in my chapter "Orfeo ed Euridice, Philology and Mercury: Marriage as Metaphor for Relationship within Composition," in *Medieval and Renaissance Humanism: Rhetoric, Representation and Reform*, ed. Stephen Gersh and Bert Roest (2003), pp. 31–54.

I express my thanks for the frequent sabbatical leaves provided by Claremont Graduate University, as well as for research funds, research assistants, and travel support attached to the Benezet Chair in the Humanities, which I hold within the department of music.

I am grateful for the stimulating input from audiences around the world who have interacted with the lines of thought expressed in this volume, as well as my colleagues within the Claremont Consortium for Medieval and Early Modern Studies; and the Center for Medieval and Renaissance Studies, University of California, Los Angeles. Many of my colleagues have read chapters, contributed valuable suggestions, and provided an environment highly conducive to intellectual and collegial endeavors.

Finally, I wish to express my heartfelt gratitude to my students in the numerous and diverse university situations over many years—including at Indiana University; the Schola cantorum Basiliensis and University of Basel Institute of Musicology; University of North Carolina, Chapel Hill; California State University, Northridge; Central European University, Budapest; the University of New England, Armidale, New South Wales, Australia; and finally and especially, at Claremont Graduate University and the Claremont Colleges—for probing, provocative, questions; stimulating discussions; and most of all, a refusal to be satisfied with conventional explanations. I have been most privileged to have had eager students and have greatly benefited from interactions with them.

Preface: Music, Devotion, Emotion, and Intellection

This volume addresses the problem of music and composition in an anonymous creative milieu, which could very well be the greatest impediment to understanding medieval music today. We have other examples of this problem of anonymous composition, for example, in the *Glossa ordinaria,* the large-scale medieval commentary on the Bible, produced largely by commentators who, even with the best of efforts at identifying them, have for the most part remained anonymous.[1] But the problem is crucial for medieval music in relation to the medieval concept of "fame," as well as the basic concept of what a "composer" is and does—as well in relation to the concepts of "creative originality" and "inspiration." One might go so far as to remark that the medieval conceptualization of the creative process differs significantly in every conceivable way from the concept of creative work, as well as the composer, during the last two centuries, as well as today. Both the compositional process and ways in which this process differs significantly from what is normally assumed today have not, to my knowledge, been adequately explained. This book fills this gap and also supplies an urgently needed textbook for medieval music for the undergraduate university audience, the graduate student in medieval studies, as well as for the professional musicologist and medievalist.

Despite commonly held views of the creative process, the anonymous medieval artistic milieu is difficult to assess with the proper degree of understanding and appreciation. Accordingly, widely used and repeatedly published histories of music have often relied upon anachronistic, uncritically accepted assumptions of the so-called composer, such as Leonin, Perotin, and Franco of Cologne, who single-handedly "created" compositions for which much must be accepted in terms of music historical lore that has accrued through the years.[2] In my years of teaching both undergraduates and graduates in music, as well as interdisciplinary medieval studies; giving papers; and fielding the questions that have ensued, I have noticed that most textbooks on medieval music currently used today are nearly incomprehensible for music students and medievalists alike.[3] These textbooks, still widely used, were in fact written several decades ago and, therefore, have not taken into consideration the recently burgeoning fields of medieval studies. Many assumptions are made, jargon is used frequently, and uncritically accepted historigraphical agendas from the earlier decades of the 20th century (such as "schools," and most of all, the prevalent recourse to "form" to solve nearly every explanatory problem) relied on. This volume aims to present a mentality based on the education received during the Middle Ages; the texts that were read; and the principles, concepts, formulations, and vocabulary that proceeded directly from them. As the Oxford medieval historian and exegete of medieval biblical literature Beryl Smalley, remarked, "They all read the same books." In an age of increased specialization and rigidly focused professional training, our own intellectual environment is more scattered, nor, in spite of the aims of the increasingly popular field of interdisciplinary studies, is shared reading a trend today. The topics that follow give indication of priorities, as well as goals in bringing medieval music into a present intellectual milieu in terms of understanding, teaching, and experiencing music in performance.

Most of all, *The Cultural Context of Medieval Music* attempts to bring into focus *medieval* priorities with respect to music. Music in the Middle Ages (very broadly interpreted to the late 18th century), rather than existing solely for its educative or entertainment value, or as self-expression of the individual artist and composer, had the serious challenge of exemplifying the basic concepts that underlie the universe, as well as being perceptible in everyday life in the world. These basic principles include the concepts of particularity—particular things—within general, unlimited, inchoate mass, relationship, and movement. Far more than a luxury or entertainment, music as a discipline was utterly necessary within the medieval educational system, as well as within the mentality of every reflective individual in the Middle Ages. The importance of music as a powerful educational tool was also enhanced by the fact that one *sang* these principles. Each day in monastic and cathedral schools, in chapels, and in churches, one experienced *particular* tones (as one sang them, one discrete tone after the other); *connection* (as one progressed from one tone to the next); and the nature of *movement* (as one sang through an entire Introit, for example, or even more obviously in the case of the melismatic, nearly textless Alleluia in which one could not help be aware of the passage of time and sound through the experience of the movement of one's own voice). Augustine's mandate that learning must be delightful, attractive, as well as experiential and comprehensible, was fulfilled.

This process of bringing medieval priorities to bear on medieval music is a departure from other recent music history textbooks and monographs in which 20th-century priorities such as "form" and "style," are primary. For the most part, these textbooks were written earlier on in the 20th century by musicologists who had not read the contextual primary and secondary literature of the Middle Ages, had no comprehension of medieval education, and were not research scholars of the Middle Ages. Many had never had more than superficial contact with manuscripts containing medieval music. Many of the widely used histories of music that have been available for more than a half century were not authored by scholars who had direct knowledge even of liturgical manuscripts, let alone its surrounding intellectual context. Hence, a 20th-century context often served as backdrop for medieval music, and modern specialties have divided what would have been—and was in fact—a unified educational and mental culture in which music played an indispensable part.

That music can be used as an example, also for 20th-century priorities, gives an important clue to its disciplinary function as an exemplary discipline, namely, that it works. Music by its nature, using the invisible substances of time, sound, and motion, makes concepts, even ideology plain—be it the concept of *figura in modis,* a medieval priority and apt tool; the notion of a great composer composing great works; or the notion of "form" in music (20th-century priorities). Music bares intellectual, ideological, and cultural attributes, making them comprehensible, available to experience, often understandable to logical and conventional process, and is, most of all, attractive, even *delicious* to the taste. We will trace each medieval attribute, matching it with its musical exemplification, for an understanding of music in its intellectual, liturgical, emotional—in other words, the *human* context of the Middle Ages.

NOTES

1. *Glossa ordinaria,* see Beryl Smalley, *The Study of the Bible in the Middle Ages,* who opened up the problem of identities in an essentially anonymous medieval authorial milieu. Palémon Glorieux mentioned that the intellectual community at the early University of Paris in the first half of the 13th century was engaged in a commentary to replace the *Glossa ordinaria* but gives no further support for this statement; see *Répertoire des Maîtres en théologie de Paris au XIIIe siècle,* 2 vols. (Paris, 1933–1934), especially introduction to vol. 1.

2. Cf. fifth edition of the *Grove's Dictionary of Music and Musicians*, 9 vols., ed. Eric Blom (London, 1954) with the more recent *The New Grove Dictionary of Music and Musicians,* ed. Stanley Sadie (London, 1980), for information on how much has been passed on from one generation of writers to the next, even from the late 19th century to the present. See also discussion of Franco of Cologne in Nancy van Deusen, *Theology and Music at the Early University: The Case of Robert Grosseteste and Anonymous IV* (Leiden, 1995), pp. 75, 202.

3. I am referring, for example, to Donald J. Grout, *A History of Western Music* (New York, l960); Gustave Reese, *Music in the Middle Ages* (New York, l940); and several other more recent contributions to the music textbook industry in the English language, primarily for the large undergraduate courses of universities in the United States—a substantial commercial enterprise, but one that has been at least partially responsible for extreme conservatism in how Western music history is related to generations of American undergraduate and graduate students.

1

Introduction: Principles, Vocabulary, Concepts

Music in the Middle Ages was closely related to and made comprehensible by life experience. Not at all a dry academic field, far removed from what people did and thought about all day long, music as a discipline bridged the gap between learning and life, and as such had intense relevance to the way one lived and thought about the world. Let us examine the medieval priorities we have mentioned by observing how the concepts of *mass, portion* (chunk), particular *figura,* and *connection*/relationship, as well as *motion,* can be found in what might appear, on the surface, to be a folktale. (Read it carefully, with patience, since these priorities are imbedded within the story. Priorities are unlocked only with effort.) The story brings out, one by one, through repetition, all that is necessary to understand key aspects of a medieval mentality toward composition with music and words.

NOVELLA 59: "FIORDINANDO"

According to 19th-century compiler Gherardo Nerucci, this story was told to him by one Giovanni Becheroni, a farmer (*contadina*). In the following English translation, capitalizations have been retained from the original edition of Nerucci, since each *figura* indicated by a uppercase letter delineates a recognizable and consistent type within the entire group of *figurae,* or "varied and diverse characters." Phrase lengths and punctuation within the original Italian have also been retained for the most part, to communicate the conversational tone of the narrative. This English translation has retained the nuances of Nerucci's Italian text, which also includes shifts between past and present tenses.

> In the old days, a King had a son called Fiordinando, who almost never left his room but went on reading and studying. He would go out of

his room to have breakfast, lunch, to walk a bit in the garden; and afterwards, he would shut himself up in his room with his books. The King had at his service a competent young man as a hunter and this man brought to the palace lots of good game everyday. And it happened that this hunter once said to the King, "Would you be pleased, your Majesty, if I went to pay a visit to master Fiordinando? I haven't seen him for many months." "Go and visit him. It may give my good son some diversion from his studies." The hunter then went to Fiordinando's room. When Fiordinando saw him, quite suddenly, he asked, "What sort of work are you doing in court, wearing those big boots?" The young man answered, "I am the hunter of the King, the one who delivers fowl, hares, and such animals killed in the forest, to the noble table." "But is hunting a pleasant pastime?" Fiordinando asked; and the young man answered, "Oh yes, most certainly, especially if you have a passion for it." "Alright," said Fiordinando. "I shall try it myself. Don't say anything so as to give the impression that you put me up to it. I shall ask my father to see if he will let me come with you one of these mornings." The young man says, "What? Do not be afraid. I won't say a word. When you are ready, I shall be at your command."

The [next] day after breakfast, Fiordinando said to the King, "Do you know what, Father? I have read a book about hunting, and it pleased me so much that I would like to try out this pastime. Will you permit this?" "Do as you please," answered the King, "But be careful, because hunting can be dangerous. I shall give you as your companion my hunter, because he is very good and knows his trade perfectly well."

So one fine morning as the sun rose, Fiordinando and the hunter mount their horses, armed to the teeth, and leave the city for the thick brush far from habitation; and they set themselves to the task without delay, so that by noon they had themselves so many animals lying on the ground that they were not able to carry them away on their backs. So they called to a local wood-cutter, gave him this burden with the express order to carry it to the palace, and with the message that they would probably not return because they intended to carry on with their pastime. So then after quickly feeding themselves (restoring themselves with food and wine), Fiordinando and the hunter again wandered around in the wood, and they are so very enthusiastic in running about after the game that when it became dark, they simply got lost—one here, the other there—and although they tried to find each other by shouting, it was useless. They could not find one another, and that was that.

In the darkness of the night, Fiordinando, tired and exhausted—both he and his horse—got down from the saddle to rest and sat down at the foot of a tree, preoccupied because of getting lost. At that moment Fiordinando believed that he could see some sort of a light at half a mile's distance amongst the tangled vegetation. So with that, he grasped his horse by the rein and set off towards the light, and arrived at a large square where there was a beautiful, seigniorial mansion, where at a large open gate, a horrible and truly ugly monster was standing with a torch in his hand. Both astonished and suspicious, Fiordinando went up to the monster and asked him whether he could sleep there for the night. The monster did not open his mouth, but with a nod, indicated to Fiordinando to follow him, first took him to the stables to house his horse, and then led him upstairs to a drawing room with lit fire, refreshments, and a heap of cigars. And without proffering a word, the monster left Fiordinando in complete freedom to do as he wished.

After a little more than an hour, when Fiordinando had already drunk some wine and smoked a few cigars, the monster returns, indicating with a movement of his hand for Fiordinando to get up; and Fiordinando followed him to a salon which looked just like an enchanting dream. From the balcony over the set table were hanging chandeliers in massive gold, large as baskets; the cutlery, plates, and glasses were of gold and silver, the table cloth and napkins were silk embroidered with pearls and diamonds. Altogether everything was marvelous, so that your eyes seemed to pop right out of your head just looking at it. But since Fiordinando was very hungry, he did not stand around to gape, but sat right down in a large armchair to eat; then he suddenly heard the rustle of garments descending the stairs, and turned his face and saw a Queen with her retinue of twelve ladies-in-waiting entering the room. This Queen was young and inexpressibly beautiful, and was wearing a veil on her head that covered half her face; and she did not say a word. The ladies-in-waiting did not say anything either. They remained mute, but they lifted her and set her upon a large, upholstered, chair next to Fiordinando; and then both he and the Queen began to eat. Still silent, nobody opened their mouths during the dinner, and when they had finished, the ladies-in-waiting accompanied the Queen to her rooms.

Fiordinando really did not know what to think of such an extraordinary event, and although he very much wanted to find out the mystery of the palace, this was impossible to figure out because of the silence that reigned within. When the monster reappeared with the lit torches and gave him a sign to follow him, Fiordinando went with him to a princely chamber designated for his rest that night. The monster put one of the torches in a chandelier, and left Fiordinando to his own devises.

Fiordinando undressed and climbed into the bed, but as soon as he had settled between the sheets, a secret door opens and the Queen enters with her twelve ladies-in-waiting. Fiordinando, seeing this with an elbow propped up on the cushions, was watching for what was going to happen next. And the ladies-in-waiting at that moment undressed the Queen except for her head-veil, put her in to lie beside Fiordinando, and went away. The Queen did not say a word, and fell asleep right away, so that Fiordinando, after looking at her, calmly touching her, also remained mute; and having lain down, sleep came over him so that cannons could not have been able to wake him. At dawn, the ladies-in-waiting came to dress the Queen and take her with them and a moment later when Fiordinando had already gotten up, the monster came to take him away, gave him a good breakfast, as many cigars as he wished and made him get down to the stables to his horse. And in the end, the monster gave him the sign that he was free to leave.

Without delay Fiordinando set out to look everywhere in order to find the way home and to find his companion lost the day before in the forest. But he was unsuccessful, so that when darkness came, he thought it would be better to return to the palace of that Queen, where, to keep it short, the same things happened as the first time, although on the third morning when he had gone out into the middle of the thicket he ran into the hunter and they galloped off into the city. But Fiordinando did not say anything to him about his adventures, but rather related to him some made-up stories in order to explain why they had not been able to meet for such a long time.

Upon his return home, Fiordinando appeared to be a completely changed man. He very nearly found his books boring, and he became ill-humored, lack-luster, and apathetic. His mother noticed this right away, and at once began harping at him to find out the reason for the change. Today she would talk to him, tomorrow she would question him; and finally Fiordinando revealed to her his adventures in the forest, and told her bluntly that he was desperately in love with the beautiful Queen, but did not know how to have her, especially since in two nights he was not able to get a word out of her mouth, and since everything within the palace seemed to be mute. The mother says, "Go back there for dinner and when the Queen is settled at your side, find a way somehow to throw her silverware onto the floor, and as soon as she bends down to pick it up, take away her head-veil. You will see that she will say something then."

Fiordinando took heed, saddled his horse and off he quickly rode to the palace in the forest, where he was received as usual. At dinner he behaved according to the advice of his mother and with an elbow made her silverware fall onto the floor. The Queen bent down to pick it up and at that moment Fiordinando took away the veil from her head. Upon that, the Queen rises, all angry, and exclaims, "Oh, rascal! You betrayed me! If I had been able to sleep another night with you without speaking and without unveiling myself, my destiny would have been that you would have been my spouse. But the charm has been destroyed. Now I have to go to Paris for eight days and from there to St. Petersburg, where I shall be competed for—and who knows who will be able to win me. Farewell! And you should know that I am the Queen of Portugal!"

And, suddenly, she and the palace disappeared, and Fiordinando was abandoned in the middle of the forest thicket, and he had to struggle to find his way home. He did not waste time since he wanted to look for the beautiful Queen; he took a travel bag, filled it with money, and chose a trusted man-servant to accompany him. In a post-chaise he left for Paris and without stopping, and half-dead from the exertion, he did not get down before he had reached an inn in that famous city.

When he had had some rest from his trip, with great attentiveness, he set out to discover if the Queen of Portugal had really arrived in Paris; and first of all, he wanted to know if the innkeeper had any information to that effect. He says, "Is there any news in these parts?" The innkeeper answers, "Nothing new has happened. What news should there be?" Fiordinando says, "There is news of so many different kinds: wars, festivities, famous people passing through." "Ah," exclaims the innkeeper, "Well, there is one piece of news. The Queen of Portugal has come to Paris five days ago, and in three will leave for St. Petersburg. She is a beautiful and very learned lady, and she takes pleasure in visiting the sites, and every afternoon takes a walk with twelve ladies-in-waiting outside the city gates nearby." Fiordinando asks, "Is it possible to watch her?" The innkeeper answers, "Ah, yes, since she is walking in public anyone may see her." "Good," said Fiordinando. "In the meantime prepare something to eat since we are hungry." "And how do you wish your wine? White or red?" Says Fiordinando, "Give us the best. We shall take red; it is stronger." So the host set the table, but he put in a good dose of opium so that when Fiordinando and his servant went outside the gates to wait for the Queen, they suddenly became so sleepy that they fell asleep like logs. A while later comes the Queen and sees Fiordinando, and recognizes him, but she did not manage to wake him up although she called him by his name and shook him all over. Finally, she became tired, took off a diamond from her finger, placed it on his face and went away.

Now, one should know that a few steps away amongst the trees within that place there lived a hermit in a cave, who slowly came out after the Queen had barely left, and took the ring from Fiordinando's face and quietly returned to his hideout. After some time, Fiordinando wakes up again first, and managed to get his man-servant to open his eyes by touching his face. And it was already dark. The two attributed their sleep to the exceedingly strong red wine; and since they had not noticed what had happened while they were asleep, they were angry for having lost time for running into the Queen.

The second day, the innkeeper says, "How do you want your wine today? Red or white?" "No, no," exclaims Fiordinando. "Give us white wine; it will not be so strong." But that scoundrel of an innkeeper laced the white wine with opium so that they, as usual, crashed onto the meadow. And the Queen of Portugal did not manage to rouse Fiordinando in any way, and then half-desperate, she put a lock of her hair on his face and went on her way. The hermit was watching this from his cave. Again, he picked up the hair, and when Fiordinando and his servant woke up in the darkness of the night, they had noticed nothing.

Fiordinando did not understand why this disgrace of falling asleep should keep happening, and was inclined to berate his servant. He was thoroughly annoyed by the thought of having already lost two useful days, and at the thought of having the Queen of Portugal leave for St. Petersburg without his speaking with her. He swore not to drink any more wine, but the innkeeper laced his soup with opium instead. Anyway, after reaching the meadow outside the gate on the last day, Fiordinando already felt his head getting heavy. Taking out two sawed-off pistols from his pocket, he shows them to his servant. "If you don't stay awake to attend me, these are for you. I shall empty them into your brain. Be sure of that." When he could not stand it any longer, he lay down, deep in sleep. The servant, as well, wishing to serve his master as much as he was afraid of the sawed-off pistols, did his utmost to stay awake, but to no avail so that that in the end his eyes closed and he lay down next to Fiordinando, sleeping like a log. Sometime later the Queen appears; she approaches and furiously shook Fiordinando, trying to raise him, screaming, and turning him around in the grass. And when she saw that she could not wake him up, she started to weep violently, so that instead of tears, drops of blood fell down her cheeks. She took her handkerchief and dried her cheeks; and then placed the bloodied handkerchief upon Fiordinando's face and returned to the inn, got into her carriage and went straight off to St. Petersburg.

In the meantime, the hermit came out of cave, and once again took away the handkerchief, and was watching to see what was going to happen. In the middle of the night, Fiordinando wakes up again, and, angry because of his disgrace and the disobedience of his servant, straight away takes out his sawed-off pistols and is on the point of emptying them into the brains of that poor man who was still asleep. But the hermit came out in time to stop him and said to him, "He is not guilty of what has happened. The guilty one is the innkeeper who laced the red wine, the white wine, and the soup with opium." "Oh, and how do you know this?" exclaims Fiordinando. The hermit says, "I know this because you have enemies and I know them. What you don't know is that the Queen of Portugal has come every day for three days to rouse you from your sleep and was unsuccessful. And she placed on your face a diamond, a lock of her hair, and a handkerchief stained with the blood of her bloody tears." Fiordinando asks, all surprised and sad, "Where are these things?" The hermit says, "I have the things for safe-keeping in order to avoid some thief stealing them without you noticing. Here they are; take them, keep them safe, because if you act wisely, they might make you lucky." "How?" asked Fiordinando. The hermit says, "The Queen of Portugal has already gone to St. Petersburg to be competed for, and she will become the wife of the winner. Now, with those presents hung on your lance, the knight who has them will certainly beat out everyone else. So if you think that this is a worthwhile venture, make haste now and get yourself to the tournament on time."

It is difficult to imagine in what way Fiordinando rushed by post-chaise from Paris to St. Petersburg. He actually managed to get there in time to enroll in the tournament, but not under his own name. They had built in that city a stadium with bleachers for the tournament, the prize of which was the beautiful Queen of Portugal. And famous warriors had arrived all over the world with large retinues of servants and arms shining bright as the sphere of the sun. But during the three days of the festivities, Fiordinando kept his visor down and wore at the top of his lance the diamond, the lock of hair, or the handkerchief of the Queen.

He threw down horses and knights so that they seemed like falling bats, and not one of them remained standing, so that he was proclaimed winner and husband to the Queen.

When she saw him open his visor and recognized him, she fell into her chair with great contentment. And when they had celebrated their wedding, Fiordinando and the Queen returned home and were received with celebration and joy by the court and the people.[1]

Becheroni–Nerucci's narrative is important from several points of view. First, it is significant that Fiordinando is a reader, a studier, who reads both day and night, cramming and filling up his mind as a repository with subject, images, ideas, as an invisible substance full of potential for future use. The Queen of Portugal is also "learned." The story, furthermore, is a collection of metaphors and allusions, with chunks of substance from the Old and New Testaments and classic texts, that is, the Queen's drops of blood as tears (Christ before his crucifixion whose drops of sweat became drops of blood); the sacrifice of the man-servant, halted just in time (Old Testament Abraham's sacrifice of Isaac, interrupted just at the point of Isaac's death); the cave in which the wise hermit lives (Plato's famous cave); and finally, especially, the forest, the most significant feature of the story, as we will see. The narrative takes place within the delineatory outlines of the Orpheus and Eurydice myth, in which substance-material is united with communication. How is a person who lives somewhere in the countryside of Tuscany, or Nerucci himself, to know all of this? He, or they, had been gathering in substance from many sources (as does the main figure of the tale) throughout their lives, to be brought together in discernible, identifiable, modular, chunks for their own purposes, combined accordingly to the prior-posterior order that is logical, sometimes ironic, and displays their own predilection. Let us proceed further into this process.

The story—chosen carefully as an example, not only of the subject at hand, but of allegory as a way of moving, one step at a time—is a love story, set in a far away, unspecified place, at an indeterminate time; it has been placed by collectors and folklorists into the so-called type of Cupid and Psyche, and the story also, even as read in the 21st century, shows how much vitality an imagined Middle Ages retained in the late 19th century, when Nerucci published this tale—with its kings, queens, knights, and jousts, carried out, of all places, in St. Petersburg, given the fact that the material for this story is said to have been related by a person by the name of Giovanni Becheroni, from the region of Montale Pistoiese, Tuscany. Many who have worked with such folktales can attest to the fact that these tales, together, are a material that, like all materials, contain the propensity for attraction. For example, Italo Calvino wrote with respect to the anthology of folktales that he had brought together and organized: "I could not forget, for even an instant, with what mystifying material with which I was dealing," and further, "Meanwhile, as I started to work, to take stock of the material available, to classify the stories into a catalog which kept expanding, I was gradually possessed by a kind of mania, an insatiable hunger for more and more versions and variants. Collating, categorizing, comparing became a fever."[2] Attracted by the material substance of the tales he was collecting, he reached for more and more, making his own order in the material he brought together, refashioning what he had at hand for his own purposes, much as one might work with clay or shape bread dough.

Let us look more closely at Fiordinando's story, since it contains clues for both communication and composition as well as artistic production—and a view of works of art—in the period under consideration, that is, from approximately the first generation of the 9th century to the middle of the 13th, a period commonly referred to as the Middle Ages, although one might take issue with both title as well as time spectrum, since, as we will see, this period shows a deep continuity with the past, or Late Antiquity, and the mental, analytical tools that were developed then certainly have usefulness for the present. We can find much that would have been recognizable to medieval people in our world today. One reason, for example, why the movie industry in Hollywood is so successful is that films produced there follow the constructional principles, as well as the communicational features of medieval art production—and, of course, Hollywood is still making films that depict, as our story does, a view of the Middle Ages often along the same lines. To say all this is not to hint for a moment that this story reaches back to the Middle Ages—our project here is not to search for origins or an evolutionary development. The story is clearly a composition of Nerucci, with broad outlines taken from a person, who he names, who told it to him. Rather, we will look at principles of construction the story makes clear that can be found as well in medieval works, exemplified by music. Furthermore, the story brings together *substance* with the *communication* of that substance. This is in fact the obvious point of the first half of the story.

Let us return now to specific details found in the tale. First, the story appears to be divided quite naturally into pieces of material, or *chunks* of material, of approximately the same size. This aspect has been emphasized most of all by phrases set off by punctuation, by paragraphs, and by capital letters designating significant figures, which have been retained in the English translation of the tale. This is not just a matter of outlay and conscious division into units that have been superimposed upon the material of the story. The story itself, by its very nature, or by the internal properties of the material used, divides itself into these chunks, many of which are self-contained. Each presents an autonomous transaction, action, or piece of information that is made clear by means of an indicative, revealing, gesture, phrase, description, idea, or self-contained action. The chunks also, as they occur, one by one, convey a sense of motion—of onward directionality. One is taken along, even captivated, by the way in which the story moves, chunk by chunk, and one is also, at the same time, conscious of this movement, since each chunk has a principal figure that identifies the chunk, registers the movement, and delineates both chunk and action.

Let us look at these principal figures. The King is provides a delineating, recognizable format for the opening chunk—a *figura*—to use a term that also brings out the underlying motivational aspect of the narrative passage; Fiordinando, the "reader and studier," the "hunter," the "hermit," and, of course, the "Queen." All of these figures are given shape by a delineating, characteristic feature, or by the fact that kings and queens, generally, are understood to have certain consistent features such as "kingliness" and "queenliness," dignity, largesse, and the power to give orders. There are also the delineating shapes or "figures" (*figurae*) of palace, forest, meadow, town, city, and cave, and there are delineating gestures or characteristic movements as well, of the hunter's ride into the forest, the chase of the hare, the entrance into the castle, the appearance and procession of the queen and her ladies-in-waiting, the retreat to the bed-chamber, the return homeward, and so on. It is fascinating to notice how each chunk is carefully given a distinctive, identifiable format by its own characteristic figure. In fact, the entire story, as it moves along its course, can be seen to be an "alphabet" of figures—an entire collection of "varied and diverse figures." Just as the letters of the alphabet are combined into syntax— into syllables, parts of speech, and sentences—so the varied and diverse figures of this alphabet of stock characters present themselves, either singly or combined, so that the syntax and connected motion of the narrative moves along, figure by figure.

The forest, too, is not happenstance, it would seem, since it recurs and plays a prominent part in the narrative. Into the forest the prince and the hunter ride; both are taken deeper and deeper into the forest until both hunter and prince (as the principal character) become lost in the thicket of underbrush within the deepest portion of the woods. The palace emerges suddenly within the forest; and the hermit emerges, hides behind, goes back to, and reenters the forest. The hermit also comes out of, and goes back into, the cave. All of this is told in utter simplicity so that a child can ride along with the narrative, captivated by its motion that draws one forward to the next happening, the next chunk, or module of material. The story then offers, almost without the reader's realization, an example of particular, self-contained modules (or chunks) and of the connection between these modules (expressed by the Latin *copula,* or "coupler"), as well as the motion necessary for moving from one module to the next until the movement ends, and that is the end of it.

But motion is also activated in the mind of the reader, or, rather, one can choose the particular motion one wishes to follow. In fact, one *must* choose a motion or mode of understanding. One makes a choice, in fact, whether one realizes it or not. The first, most obvious way, or *mode* (the Latin *modus*) of motion, is to take all of this at face value, or literally, and this has led, in recent times, to criticism of both medieval literature, as well as so-called folktales, as not being well-suited to the purpose of "telling it as it is" or reporting accurately. Both medieval writing and folktales are faulted for being "derivative," fanciful, fabulous, or even worse, foolish—in other words, some argue that they should not to be taken seriously as genuine historical writing worthy of credibility. Take, for example, the action in which the queen rides off in her carriage from Paris to St. Petersburg, followed posthaste by Fiordinando; such a journey, in the late 19th century, would have been an undertaking of prodigious proportions. (This is, however, an interesting feature of historical significance in our tale here, namely, that the author(s) have included a "heap of cigars" as one of the criteria for luxury that Fiordinando is invited to enjoy in the silent palace.)

Secondly, however, one can choose the manner of reading and understanding this story as a conscious "covering" for another message, a hard shell that can be pulled away or cracked only by reflection, practice, and time. One learns only gradually to do this, and one must proceed step-by-step in this endeavor. If one chooses this mode, or way of moving, with the material to be read, there is the possibility of the *outer,* confusing, tangled, forest filled with wood, with branches and underbrush all going this way and that in utter disorder, as well as the *inner* forest of the prince-reader's memory filled with all of that "stuff" he had stored there from reading all day every day. Both the forest that surrounds the castle, as well as the reader's own unordered thoughts and impressions, constitute a resource that can be accessed according to need and the competence of the hunter (outer forest), and reader (inner forest). One could ride off after game, or one could follow an idea to its conclusion, whatever that might be. In fact, as one reads this novella one has the intuitive sense that there is something else at stake—that there is more to it than what meets the eye. This, then, is the allegorical mode of reading and understanding the story, described also by the Latin term, *integumentum,* a covering, tent, or shell that needs, with patience and will, to be removed in order to get at the real significance—a meaning that somehow seems both elusive and valuable. There are small, subtle, indications, or, again, *figurae,* throughout the story that give reason for believing that the effort at discovering the hidden message is, without a doubt, worth it, just as the pearl beyond price, marrying the "Queen of Portugal" is worth every bit of exertion on the part of the prince.

One could also choose another "motion" or "way of moving" through the material of the story, a mode that would involve making the story intensely personal—applying the story to one's own time, place, and circumstances. There are nuggets of wisdom for the reader to glean and appropriate. Examples of these pieces of advice that might come in handy for one's own circumstances might be: It's better not to lose one's way in the woods. It's better not to try to deceive another person who has been kind to you. Sometimes it is better not to go after more than what has been given. One needs to carefully and attentively identify one's enemies. Still another piece of advice to be applied to daily life might be that the greater the reward, the more worthwhile the goal; the more careful, patient effort must be expended, often done in silence and without apparent progress, until the goal is reached, and one's efforts come to fruition. To force a consequence can lead to a much more circuitous pathway in the end, as was certainly true in Fiordinando's case. This mode or way of moving can be identified as the tropological mode, or one in which a "turn about" occurred. One needs to turn the features of the story, or the *figurae,* around and point that figure, as a pointing finger, at oneself. A trope, also, most commonly, was a metaphor or analogy, in which an application to oneself was implied.

But there were also glimmers of an ideal future, an aroma of the feeling that human beings possess, that there is a better world, a place, and life of beauty somewhere else. The story drops clues of this throughout, from beginning to end, of the shining palace and the queen as inexpressibly beautiful and richly learned, and the ideal of finding or connecting up with true love (Fiordinando and the Queen). This is a futuristic mode or way of moving through the verbal material, which has also been named the "eschatological mode." All of these ways, or manners of moving through the material of the story could be, and have been, called modes, with the figures of the story indicating the appropriate mode along the way. In fact, this was regarded as such a common way of composition and reception in the Middle Ages that there is a standard name for this, namely, *figurae in modis*—figures within movement. These figures also indicate the internal properties of the material of the story itself, as well as providing a means to identify each one of the blocks or chunks that serve as building blocks from which the story is made.

The story tells us a great deal, and thus serves as an example of a composition. The story is also about communication and about how human beings make or fashion artistic works, most of all, to communicate. Perhaps we should review what can be found here, for the reason that these features are exactly those that are identified by medieval writers, illuminators, and composers as well; and what has been said so far would have been readily understood by any of the above from the 9th to the 14th century—and even beyond. These features also underlie music and its important place in medieval educational, emotional, and intellectual culture.

In the first place, we have seen that an important constructional unit within the entire unordered, even inchoate, mass of possibilities—also of sound, should the story be read aloud—is what we have called the self-contained chunk, or module, the Latin *punctum,* a translation of the Greek *cento.* The novella appears to be divided into these chunks from beginning to end, such as:

> In the old days, a King had a son called Fiordinando, who almost never left his room, but went on reading and studying.

> So one fine morning as the sun rose, Fiordinando and the hunter mount their horses, armed to the teeth, and leave the city for the thick brush far from habitation, and they set themselves to the task without delay, so that by noon they had themselves so many animals lying on the ground that they were unable to carry them.

> The monster did not open his mouth, but with a nod, indicated to Fiordinando to follow him.

> And without proffering a word, the monster left Fiordinando in complete freedom to do as he wished.

> Without delay Fiordinando set out to look everywhere in order to find the way home and to find his companion lost the day before in the forest.

> Now, one should know that a few steps away amongst the trees within that place, there lived a hermit in a cave, who slowly came out after the Queen had barely left, and took the ring from Fiordinando's face and quietly returned to his hideout.

Although these chunks are self-contained, they are not placed in random order, the Latin *ordo.* In fact, order as well as the unseen, even mysterious, connection between the chunks is of much importance for the forward motion of the narrative. This order is reinforced by indications of "before" and "after," prior and posterior, such as: "The second day, the innkeeper says, 'How do you want your wine today? Red or white?'" In other words, the material of time is constructed within the story into discernible portions or chunks as modules, and these chunks follow one another in an order that can be recognized as making sense, since the chunks also use time as a material in an arrangement of succession: before and after.

We see also that the chunks are differentiated from one another by characteristic figures (*figurae*) that delineate one important, characteristic aspect of each chunk. By keeping track of the figures, we can, as readers, keep track of the chunks so that the story makes sense, that is, follows along in an orderly and logical fashion. In a way, the *figurae* themselves analyze the chunks, in that they clearly bring out what is essential, worth remembering. This is enhanced within the Italian text in terms of capital letters. The *figurae*, at the same time, indicate movement step-by-step in the order of the narrative. These *figurae* include, in the order of their appearance: (1) the King of long ago; (2) Fiordinando, the reader, who is the only figure who has a name; (3) the king's hunter, who is passionate about his profession of hunting game in the forest; (4) the Queen, whose face is covered with a veil, and who is also mute; (5) 12 ladies-in-waiting who are not delineated further except that they perform occasional tasks, such as following the Queen, or settling her in her upholstered chair, that is, they are delineated or characterized by their movements (in other words, their movements give them a role); (6) Fiordinando's mother, presumably the king's wife, who is clever and tricky, and pesters her son; (7) the innkeeper who is a "scoundrel"; and (8) the hermit who lives in a cave and who hides behind trees. Each *figura* has at least one articulating identifying characteristic that indicates a particular place within the narrative. These outward characteristics, be it of profession, activity, or speech, are connected to internal emotional substances (such as prince-reader's "love" of learning, which is replaced by his love for the Queen), resulting in an energy, the Latin *virtus motiva*, that motivates that figure. But, again, the prince-reader is the only *figura* to have a name.

Together—should one imagine the lot of them, and one must do this, since they never all come together in one place at one time—they all constitute a colorful band of varied and diverse *figurae* (the Latin would be *figurae variarae* or *characterae variarae*). They are all from different stations of life, as well as different professions, such as queen, hunter, hotel manager, and recluse. Together, as well as separately, by means of the ways in which they actualize their inner propensities, given them, presumably, by birth (such as the king), as well as by characteristic gestures, and the phrases that they utter, each lends a differentiating identity to the chunk in which he or she occurs. It can also be the case that a figure arbitrates an event. One could say this another way: each *figura* shapes the object into which it is enclosed. They all, appearing in the story one after the other, provide a whole group of possibilities to the one who places together these chunks, that is, the composer of the words, music, or drawings.

But that is not all there is to it. Each *figura* is the *external* definition of *internal* properties so that the external gives notice of, as well as access to, an unseen, invisible nature that, more often than not, contains an ethical component, a moral substance, a *virtus motiva*, or invisible, motivating energy. This energy provides an unseen source of movement, manifested in deliberation, decision, and action within each one of our varied and diverse figures. The kingly figure delineates stability and dignity (*dignitas*); the prince, potential (*potencia*); the hunter, passion, exploration, strength, action, and competence (*capacitas*); the prince's mother, curiosity (*curiositas*); the Queen of Portugal, resolve (*fortitudo*); the innkeeper, moral turpitude (*invidia*); and the hermit, wisdom (*sapiencia, prudencia*). Connection (*copula*) is possible between the outer and the inner, but there is also a *copula* between the *internal* properties of at least two of the *figurae*, resulting, eventually, in the uniting, as well, of the *outer figurae* of Fiordinando and the Queen. The story, in fact, is about overt connections—between the king and his subject (the hunter), the prince and his reading material, and so on—until we come at last to the concluding connection, or *copula*, between the united prince and the queen. Common internal properties are united with outer *figurae*, and the story comes to an end. Not all, however, is on the surface, and so there is room for each and every reader to be engaged with the outer *figurae*, as well as inner substance as one reads this novella. (It is significant that Nerucci has entitled this story as a "novella," that is, a composition.)

Objects, too, are *figurae* that identify and mark out each component of this narrative: first of all, the forest, into which one is led, in which one attempts to find one's way, out of which one comes, totally changed, transformed, unable to return to one's former preoccupations—one's former self. The palace, the *figura* of plenty in which every need is supplied, is also transformational and therefore, exerts a profound effect. The animals as game; the monster who has a place as an object in that he never speaks, adopting, rather, a stance; the veil; the secret door; the lock of hair; the diamond ring; the handkerchief with drops of blood—all function as *figurae* in that they delineate, identify, and serve as movers in pushing along the narrative from the beginning to the end, one chunk at a time. Even silence becomes a *figura*, a delineated entity.

Finally, in this novella, the queen neither speaks nor shows her face. So, as we have seen, the story is really about connection and, above all, *communication*—about the process and capability of uniting mute and covered phenomena, or things—in this case, human things—that consist of substance and are measurable, together with directed communication that is comprised of actualization and articulation, and above all, *sound*. Material that is patently visible but silent needs to be communicated, so that we can learn something from it, as the queen must be released from a "spell" so she can communicate and show her face.

The project of communication is the great medieval project. We find it also in the story of Orpheus and Eurydice, retold again and again in the Middle Ages, in which Eurydice (as silent material substance) is banished to the underworld as the direct result of her death, thus becoming not only silent, but unseen. Orpheus, who is the "voice," goes off searching for her, and it is nip-and-tuck with dangers, toils, and, above all, snares, until he finds her, bringing her up to the surface of the earth in some versions, and losing her in others. The medieval manuscript versions of this story fill a large book, and the tale of Orpheus and Eurydice serves the same purpose of disclosing the difficulties of bringing word together with substance, meaning with the material of sound, time, and motion, in Monteverdi's opera, *La favola d'Orfeo*, published in Venice in 1609, reprinted in 1615, and Offenbach's *Orpheus in the Underworld*, first performed in Paris in 1858, as well as Stravinsky's ballet *Orpheus*, produced in New York City for the first time in 1948. This particular story about the marriage of communication and material substance is unforgettable, so ubiquitous and universal the problem. It is also the problem music as a discipline exemplifies: making unseen but heard realities plain.

NOTES

1. For the Italian version of "Fiordinando," cf. G. Nerucci, *Sessanta Novelle Populari Montalesi (circondario di Pistoia)* (Florence, 1880): Novella LIX, repr. with introduction (Milan, 1977), pp. 490–497. I acknowledge with gratitude the invaluable help of the Romance languages philologist Outi Merisalo for the English translation included here.

2. Cf. *Italian Folktales*, selected and retold by Italo Calvino, trans. George Martin (Torino, 1956; English translation, New York, 1980), pp. xvi–xvii. There have been several reasons for collecting together so-called folktales, such as the perception of a source of national consciousness and the efforts of Finnish collectors to trace migrations. In this particular case, overriding features of pungent vitality and colorful expression also play a role in the importance of these tales, which attracted a great deal of interest and scholarship throughout the 19th and 20th centuries.

2

Music in a Culture of the Mind: A Medieval View of Resources, Material, and Composition

It is not by chance that the story of "Fiordinando" takes place in a forest. The setting of a forest is, in fact, a key factor throughout the story. After the comfortable, commodious, palace—where the prince had, for a time, enjoyed food, drink, cigars, a warm fire, and a good night's rest—had completely vanished, he finds himself again in the thicket of underbrush, in the darkest, thickest, part of the entire forest. This important chunk is one that we meet from the beginning of the 10th century—in Remigius of Auxerre's commentary on one of the most important and influential, although difficult to understand, books in the Middle Ages, *The Marriage of Philology and Mercury* of Martianus Capella. It is difficult today, perhaps, to understand why this work had such medieval currency, written in late Antiquity (that is, the third century C.E.) and quoted, as well as referred to, throughout the Middle Ages. But the reason may very well have been that it works over the same topic as "Fiordinando," that of uniting material substance with communication. Again, another similarity between "Fiordinando" and *The Marriage of Philology and Mercury* is that both use primarily the allegorical way of moving, or mode, and both have to do with making connections.

The title *The Marriage of Philology and Mercury* demonstrates this "marriage" between verbal communication (Mercury, the messenger), and *conceptual* substance (Philology). (This connection is also the real "point" of "Fiordinando.") The marriage of Philology and Mercury, however, is also one that occurs within and between songs, music, and words. This overarching concept of marriage or bonding is clear from the beginning lines:

> Sacred principle of *unity* amongst the gods, on you I call,
> you are said to grace *weddings* with your song;

it is said that a muse was your mother.
You *bind* the warring seeds of the world with *secret bonds*
and encourage the *union of opposites* by your *sacred embrace*.

Although the purpose of the work is open and apparent, that is, unity, *The Marriage of Philology and Mercury* otherwise certainly needs elucidation, since it is filled with *integumenta*, or covered allusions that have to be picked away at in order to set free the real "nugget" of meaning (just like the Queen in "Fiordinando," who is both veiled and silent). The topic of relationship is especially apparent in a hymn that occurs in the final chapter on "Harmony":

I worship you, O Jupiter, resounding with heavenly song; through you the sacred swirling of the heavens has set the glittering stars in predetermined motion. You, all-powerful Father of the multifarious gods, move and bind kingdoms beneath your scepter-bearing diadem, while Mind, which you instill with heavenly force, revolves the universe in ceaseless whirl.[1]

It is by no means difficult in our present culture of convenience and haste to experience both distaste and impatience at the amount of work required to wrest communication out of such a work as *The Marriage of Philology and Mercury* and unite syntax with content and meaning. These readers, who remain unidentified, can be compared to the king's wife, counseling Fiordinando to resort to trickery in order to short-circuit an apparently tedious process and compel the Queen to speak. This distaste for a work such as *The Marriage of Philology and Mercury*, which was clearly of great importance to medieval thought-culture, shows that when we attempt to understand a mentality of the Middle Ages, we are, in a sense, taking a journey into a foreign land in which our underlying assumptions cannot be taken for granted and accepted without reflection.

Again, as in "Fiordinando," *The Marriage of Philology and Mercury* also eventually comes around to the forest in a passage that would be singled out for particular notice in the Middle Ages. In fact, as in "Fiordinando," the real action and point of the story begins with the forest:

Amidst these extraordinary scenes and these vicissitudes of Fortune, a sweet music arose from the trees, a melody arising from their contact as the breeze whispered through them; for the crests of the great trees were very tall, and, because of this tension, reverberated with a sharp sound; but whatever was close to and near the ground, with drooping boughs, shook with a deep heaviness of sound; while the trees of middle size in their contacts with each other sang together in fixed harmonies of the duple (2.l), the sesquialtera (3.2), the sesquitertia (4.3) also, and even the sesquioctava (9.8) without discrimination, although semitones came between. So it happened that the grove poured forth, with melodious harmony, the whole music and song of the gods.[2]

Although not easy to understand (as an *integumentum*), this passage, occurring as it does at the beginning of the work (a place of relative importance), is of much interest for several reasons. First, the passage takes place within the forest, and setting a story in the forest, as we have seen, is by no means coincidental. Secondly, music is introduced to demonstrate how music itself by its use of sound substance illustrates and exemplifies realities that are otherwise difficult to understand. The terms "duple," "sesquialtera," "sesquitertia," and "sesquioctava" all refer to common musical intervals, the building-blocks of musical composition in Western music and other world musical cultures as well, not only in late Antiquity, and the Middle Ages, but today. The octave, the perfect fifth, the fourth, for example, show how actual musical material and the measurement of sound can both be incorporated into a treatise on communication, language, and composition, and fully exemplify what is at stake. Material sound substance (music) is combined with word, and "so it happened" that the totally different entities of invisible sound "stuff" that could be measured by proportional measurements could be "harmonized," that is, brought into concord through motion and time, with language. Thirdly, the passage seems to have been considered to be of importance, since it was quoted often and in many contexts throughout the Middle Ages. It is for that reason worth considering since it gives some indication of what medieval readers regarded as valuable. Examining this passage can provide clues to a mentality in which music and its exemplary power were paramount.

This forest in *The Marriage of Philology and Mercury* is full of trees. They are of various and diverse sizes and shapes, and one can only imagine all of them together. All these trees might be a canopy that partially obscures the sky. They may have become the fallen branches, and those close to the ground, together with the underbrush, may make up a thicket of assorted branches, dead leaves. In short, we have here before the eyes of the imagination all of the material that a forest produces, year after year. Without pathways, it is extremely difficult to make one's way. One can go around in circles, or give up, standing stock still. The forest material itself, rich a resource as this may be for a whole variety of purposes, such as making fires, furniture, houses, or, perhaps providing nuts to eat, as one walks along, can suddenly, especially if the forest closes in on one, becomes daunting, as well as confusing, if not downright dangerous.

One 10th-century writer, Remigius of Auxerre, in his highly influential commentary on this very passage, brought the forest to mind as a rich resource that attracted attention, inviting appropriation.[3] On the other side of the time-frame we have set for ourselves as the Middle Ages, the 14th-century writer Dante, expresses the other point of view—the forest as incoherent and confusing—in the opening lines of his great epic work concerning the course of the world, and the ways of God and man:

> When in the midst of my course of life,
> I found myself in a dark opaque forest,
> and found that I had lost my way . . ."
> (*Nel mezzo del cammin di nostra vita*
> *mi ritrovai per una selva oscura*
> *che la diritta via era smarrita ...*)

Here, Dante's "dark, opaque forest" is the forest of a clutter of material possibilities, the undergrowth of myriad thoughts, the tangled branches that obscure the sky, blocking out the light. Surely, as he wrote this, Dante was certainly aware of the fact that the scriptures of Old and New Testaments together had often been described as a dark, opaque thicket, full of possibilities in which one could easily lose one's bearings and sense of direction. In this rich resource of infinite possibilities available to him, the task that Dante had set before himself, as with any medieval writer or composer, was that of helping himself to the material at his disposal, selecting various and diverse *figurae*, and finding a way—with time, patience, and hard work—through the tangled thicket of thoughts, memories, and knowledge, taken from a lifetime of reading others' thoughts. The forest represents the unlimited possibilities that, although largely unseen, were available to the composer. The writer or composer then, as well as today, is a "connector" or "coupler" of words with conceptual substance, faced continuously with the difficult task of persuasively uniting communication with the material to be communicated. Both passages, Remigius's commentary on Martianus Capella's *The Marriage of Philology and Mercury*, and the opening phrases to Dante's *Inferno* of *The Divine Comedy*, have, directly, as their basis, a term and concept central to the *Timaeus* of Plato, the only work of this author that was accessible to, and therefore known by, a Latin-reading audience during the medieval period, at least until the *Phaedo* and the *Meno* of Plato were also translated by Henricus Aristippus, a Sicilian, in the mid-12th century. It is worth noting here that we do know what medieval people had on their minds to a large extent, since, for the most part, they all read the same books, and they wrote about what they had read—without bothering to repeat themselves concerning their primary-school education every time they wrote, which would have been tedious and, above all, unnecessary.[4] Plato's *Timaeus* is about *making things*, about fabrication incorporated into composition, and about from what substance compositions, including and especially the world itself, are made.

Of what stuff is the world made? asks Plato in the *Timaeus*. Of formless, inchoate, unlimited substance, is the answer, the Greek *hyle*, a term comparable to the concept presented in Genesis, which states that the world was without individual shapes, was void, and darkness covered the earth. *Hyle*, a term as amorphous as one could possibly imagine, is, however, presented in concrete terms in the Latin translation that a translator by the name of Chalcidius made, either at the end of the fourth or the beginning of the fifth century. Few specifics about this important translator are known, but what he thought about *hyle* is carefully delineated, since Chalcidius perceived the necessity to justify his choice of a Latin equivalent to *hyle*. Chalcidius, whoever he may have been, from whatever native country, translated the Greek *hyle* into the Latin *silva*, and he wrote 73 pages to explain the correctness and importance of his decision.

Hyle, for the translator Chalcidius, is *chaos*. The Latin word he selects to replace the Greek term, *silva*, is a perfectly ordinary noun meaning "forest"—a forest full of trees. This seems to be a commonplace substitution of one language for another, but, in fact, the choice of *silva*, a forest, rather than another possibility, such as Cicero's *substantia*, or substance, puts forward a mental image that remained for centuries. It is, of course, the mental picture of the forest, as an utterly concrete, real, repository for material of all kinds—the material from which the world was made, but material that was, as well, invisible, such as sound, time, motion, and thought. In substituting the Latin word for "a forest full of wood, brush, and trees," for a Greek term that meant everything and nothing, that is, "unformed, unlimited, matter," Chalcidius in a sense de-spooked a notion of the substance of the world, as well as the invisible substance of which thoughts were made. In connecting by one word, *silva*, both seen and unseen material (the Latin *anima*), Chalcidius brought the two together, making them manageable because unseen substance, such as thought or sound, could be imagined in very concrete terms. What did one do with wood? One set about to construct things with it, chunk by chunk, and to rationally conceive of *figurae*, as identifiable, linear indicators of substance and motion, whether material or conceptual. Through this thought process, reinforced by translational fiat, the conclusion could be reached that one could work with unseen substance in exactly the same ways as with seen, visible substance. One could shape sound in terms of blocks of sound—or chunks—exactly as if one were carving up blocks of wood. This is an astonishing thought, but from it proceeds a raison d'être for music as an exemplary discipline in Late Antiquity and the Middle Ages, since music also shapes the substances of sound, time, and motion.

Silva, a forest full of trees, is a rich source of material that can be grown up from seeds, cut down and appropriated, carved into figures, made into furniture, shaped, manipulated, piled up, and finally burnt up into heat and light. And at the end of the approximate century of their lifetimes, trees, depending upon their inner properties, die, fall to the ground, enrich the soil, and generate yet another kind of material to be used still another time. The forest contains, in a sense participates in, proclivities and properties, potential, and unlimited possibilities for generation, as well as decay, corruption, and renewal. The forest is continuously changing. Indeed, Chalcidius's metaphor of the forest, and his choice of just that expression within what by then was a philosophical discourse within the Greek language, transformed an ambiguous, vague, concept—*hyle*—and channeled it into a mental image that could make, for medieval minds, an image of construction and juxtaposition; an orderly setting in place and formation. A composer with words, images, or musical sound in the Middle Ages was above all a craftsman, a joiner of materials, respecting the material properties of these materials, and faithfully, persistently, working with them in order to bring out these material properties.

Silva, then, as a translation of the Greek term for chaos in Plato's *Timaeus,* stood for material, both seen and unseen, without limitation— a dark, even opaque, disorderly thicket; a maze; an intense, compact texture full of potentially useful stuff, inviting those who knew of its existence and who could indeed work with its material properties, to enter and help themselves to whatever was available. And, of course, forests existed all over medieval Europe, as they exist today, as examples of exactly what Chalcidius had presented, offering to a Latin readership an everyday, thoroughly relevant vision of the compositional task. It was a vision that in many cases surrounded them. The French historian Fernand Braudel in his book *The Identity of France* mentions these forests of medieval France that remained in place well into the 17th century, as full of material, as well as possibilities for lodging; some of the forests were simply available for those who otherwise had neither income nor a place to live—the homeless and fugitives from the law. He writes that "these silent, dark, forests with their piled up logs" were limitless in that they often reached over county boundaries, and there were few paths and roads.[5]

The concept of a forest as full of possibility remained in the mind of a person during period of what is commonly known as the European

Middle Ages. The concept of a forest of material from which to carve out chunks and place them together is a concept that would have automatically presented itself to a medieval imagination, simply by reading, understanding, and using, the Latin word *silva*. It was impossible to escape the literal, concrete implications of a term with such concrete implications, just as it is impossible to escape the connotations, or indeed the mental image, of "forest" in the English language, no matter what else that word might imply. So why was this, in the translator's mind, worth defending? Why spend so much time on making just that point of the substitution of one Latin word for a Greek? Chalcidius pointed to the equivalence of seen and unseen material. One could work in much the same way with both the wood of the forest, chunk by chunk, log by log, and with unseen material, such as sound. Sound, then, as a forest full of material, could be appropriated, accessed, and fashioned as well as manipulated, piece by piece into compositions; placed together in fitting and appropriate ways, artfully bringing about connection. The choice of substance to be used, as well as the connections obtained, indicated mastery. This could also be accomplished with words. The two, words and music, then, were ways of working with the same invisible materials—sound, time, and motion. Furthermore, the connection one sought was that of communication—of bringing together *sound* material ("voice" or the Latin *vox*) with *significance* (*materia/substantia,* "thing" or the Latin *res*) and making this known.

The concept of forest provides us with a key to understanding construction and composition within areas such as literature, art, and music—fields that are normally separated today, but which are united at the crux of the matter by the notion of *silva*, a forest full of material potentiality on the one hand, but also by the notion "what is already there"—*materia/substantia/natura*—that is present when one begins the task of composition. It is preexistent substance, no matter how or where one finds it. Let us see how this important concept was repeatedly invoked and worked over, and let us look at this concept's multivalent influence. Let us investigate what this medieval forest contained in terms of specific possibilities as a background for composition and communication.

NOTES

1. *Martianus Capella and the Seven Liberal Arts* II: *The Marriage of Philology and Mercury,* trans. William Harris Stahl and Richard Johnson, with E. L. Burge (New York, 1977), p. 353.
2. *The Marriage of Philology and Mercury,* pp. 9–10.

3. Cf. Remigius of Auxerre's commentary on this passage: *Commentum in Martianum Capellam,* libri I–II, ed. Cora E. Lutz (Leiden, 1962–1965), p. 86f.

4. Medieval reading is the focus of Beryl Smalley, *The Study of the Bible in the Middle Ages* (repr. Notre Dame, Indiana, 1964, third printing, 1978). One thread that runs throughout this seminal study is that this reading/studying and writing should not necessarily be placed in anachronistic post–19th-century disciplinary categories; the medieval authors and commentators were not necessarily themselves "doing philosophy" when they commented on the Bible—despite dealing with the basic questions of "how to know."

5. Fernand Braudel, *The Identity of France* (New York, 1992) I. pp. 55; 146–153, with subtitles: "The forest: jewel among properties," "The forest: a world upside down," and "The forest as refuge." In addition to the novella with which we began, collections of folktales, such as those of the Grimm brothers, often begin with a line such as: "Near a large forest lived a poor woodcutter with his wife and two children." Such openings signal that out of the forest (i.e., a remote place teeming with possibility) differentiation in terms of individual characters can be constructed. Cf. also Eugen Weber, "What is Real in Folk Tales," in *My France: Politics, Culture, Myth* (Cambridge, MA, 1991), pp. 75–91. The concrete exemplification of this concept of *silva* as a disorderly limitless mass of material that could be accessed and was available—even when invisible—would have been well-known to a Latin readership even much later than the Middle Ages. In a sense, collections of folktales themselves comprised a *silva*—a mass of material—to be appropriated. What is there—as a preexistent substance—could be appropriated, even if it had already been worked over, in some cases anonymously.

3

What Did This Medieval "Forest" Contain? Preexistent Substance, Unlimited Possibilities

What substance was in this forest (*silva*), and what had medieval composers, artists, and writers accumulated to be used at will and in many different ways?[1] All of these concepts, to a certain extent, came together in a conscious choice during the process of translation—as we have seen—that also radically altered how one thought about "stuff" and eventually, as we will see, how one, as a writer, composer, painter, or illuminator painting on the parchment of manuscripts, thought about one's work: the compositional process itself. The notion of a forest full of trees that could be selected and used infiltrated all of the work one did with words, sounds, and paint. Some of these materials, of course, could be seen and felt, weighed and measured. Other materials were made of unseen substance: the material of sound is the best example. In this repository of materials and substance, the master craftsman selected what was most useful. How one regards material, especially unseen material, is crucial here.

What substance was in this *silva*? What had people living between the 9th and the 14th centuries accumulated to be used as they wished? Here are some of the most important concepts and ideas, selected from a truly vast "forest" of material available to the composer, either with words or with sound. The "stuff" of sound, the nature of stuff, as well as the stuff of nature, are all preoccupations of writers within the period that we are considering, and we will attempt to find out what they thought about making compositions, performing them—even the act of thinking about the material to be worked over, both beforehand and in retrospect.

Well-known writers from Latin antiquity, such as Virgil, Cicero, Quintilian, and Augustine, and the translator of the *Timaeus*, Chalcidius, all contributed to the concepts we have been working with, such as *chunk,* or building block, the Greek *cento,* translated into the Latin *punctum, figurae* as delineating features of each building block, and the eventual bringing together of many chunks into a composition. All of these authors lived and worked before the period that we are expressly considering here, but their works, and the concepts contained within these highly influential works, together constituted this great repository of conceptual "trees." We will look again at the notion of *chunk* (Latin *punctum*) as a manageable piece of conceptual material that could be fitted appropriately by means of a carefully crafted coupler (the Latin *copula*).

We begin with Cicero. It is indicative of his importance and fame, both during his own lifetime and later, well, in fact, into the Common Era, that we know exactly when Cicero was born, that is, on January 3, 106 B.C.E. He was an orator and had been trained to communicate by means of sound substance contained in, and limited by, words, as well as being very much aware of their movement and the impact they could have upon an audience. Cicero was one author who had filled the repository of this medieval forest of material, and Latin readers continued to regard him as one of the most important authors to be read well after the end of the 14th century.[2] From Cicero, first of all, medieval minds received what they knew and thought of Orpheus, as well as Homer, as "makers of fables," and Pythagoras, who taught and, according to Cicero, attracted to himself a brotherhood of disciples, and whose alleged doctrines continued to be of much influence on future philosophical discourse. Cicero not only mentioned these writers, but often, as in his work *The Nature of Gods,* he gave some explanatory details that enabled readers to remember these "makers of fables."[3] In other words, Cicero made Homer, as well as Pythagoras, a "figure." But one of the most important contributions Cicero made was that of the mental construction of a discrete, enclosed interval or space of time, which he labels as an "occasion" or event in which features (*figurae*) are, so to speak, glued to a predetermined chunk of time according to their appropriateness. These features may be features composed of sound, as (to use Cicero's expression) "varieties of voices," as well as varieties of odors and touch that adhere to "an occasion." It is important to hear Cicero's voice (given here in English translation instead of the original Latin) in what he has to say to us on this subject:

> *Time* in the sense in which we now use it—for to define it absolutely and in general terms is difficult—time is a *part* of eternity definitely indicated as of a certain length, that is, a year, month, day or night. Under this category not only are past events examined, and of these past events those which have either lost their significance through lapse of time or seem incredible so that now they are regarded as fables, and those which though they occurred long ago, and are remote from our recollection

still impress us as having been correctly reported because definite re-cords of them are still to be read in literature, and those which have oc-curred recently so that most people know them, but also those things which exist in the present moment and are most certainly going on, and thirdly, actions which are to follow, of which it is possible to consider what will come to pass sooner and what later. Likewise, generally, in ex-amining time, the length of time has to be taken into consideration. For often it is appropriate to measure the action in terms of time and to see whether such an important action, or such a number of undertakings could be accomplished in a set and given time. One also takes into con-sideration the time of the year, that is the season, the month, the day, the night, the time of day or night *and any part of these.*[4]

An *occasion*, then, for Cicero, is a *part* (or chunk) of time having the convenient opportunity for doing or not doing something. And each part of time differs from the other, and according to this difference, a confined space of time can be said to be in one or the other mode. Cicero goes on to say many other things and to put occasions as con-tained parts of time into various and diverse categories; two obser-vations should be made here. First of all, Cicero seems to be treating time not as money but as material to be imagined as self-contained, different parts, or, in the language we have used, chunks of time. Sec-ondly, these chunks both move and adhere to actions or properties that cause them to differ one from the other in noticeable ways. Finally, this discernible movement can be seen to be according to ways of mov-ing or modes that we notice as occurring in a now distant, as Cicero states, "fabulous" or mythical past that is, must be, in some way, fig-ured out, or, in other words, delineated; these modes also occur in the present mode and thus are readily accessible to all. These chunks will also occur—due to the movement that is implied—sometime in the future. We have here once again what we noticed in "The Enchanted Castle," that is, movement or mode that can be taken literally because it is immediately relevant and easily understood, movement that must be discerned, that is, the inner meaning is not immediately available to what we call common sense, the mode or motion that has to do with oneself personally, or the mode of the future. Cicero is writing then of the literal, the allegorical, the tropological, as well as the eschatologi-cal modes or "ways of movement," preserved in common parlance today as *modus vivendi* or *modus operandi*. In any case, this particular concept of a *chunk* or self-contained interval of time to which features or figures that are extracted from limitless, unseen, substance adhere, is a fundamental concept throughout the Middle Ages. We will soon see how this concept of interval could be, and was, exemplified, par-ticularly in music.

Cicero made clear the possibility, indeed the obligation in rhetoric, of *shaping* and constructing time and sound as material. In shaping sound as one would a block of wood, one could also maintain control over this material. Quintilian (born between 30 and 35 C.E.) knew Cicero's work; he frequently quotes him, shaping a vivid *persona* of Cicero for his own generation as well as for hundreds of years thereafter. Quintilian's Cicero was, according to his own statement, brought together as a constructed composite of distinctive features, first in Quintilian's imagination, and then in his writing, the influence of which particularly on the Middle Ages has not yet been adequately assessed. Quintilian, who was also an orator, writing four books of instruction for future lawyers, among them his own son, goes even further than Cicero, whom he considered to be his mentor, in using and building upon this concept of a *chunk* of time-substance. This enclosed part of time (*punctum*) was just about as long as what one could speak in one breath, he wrote, and that usually contained just about as much conceptual substance as one could retain in one's mind at once. Further, Quintilian, although he uses the word *silva* only once, toward the end of his lengthy textbook on rhetoric, brings this particular expression into the context of material, writing of the person who sits down and makes an impetuous and rapid draft, as Quintilian writes, "outside of time," *ex tempore.* The sense of this passage is that this person, to whom Quintilian refers, throws at his reader a wad of material, so to speak, rather than patiently selecting through the material of his or her thoughts, pruning and honing, casting away what is inappropriate and awkward, and, at last, bringing together pieces of thought-material that have been carefully worked over. This "wad," then, is "out of time" since it occurs "all at once," rather than moment by particular moment, strand by strand, in which thought, word, and self-contained moment are all united. Quintilian goes on in this passage to write of composition and of weeding through a "congestion" of material in order to prune out exactly what it is that one needs and wants to say.[5]

We have two concepts here. Both of them, perhaps unfamiliar today, are extremely influential for composition and communication throughout the Middle Ages. The first concept is of the single moment that can be self-contained, delineated, and made particular by means of some differentiating marker, or *figura.* The second concept is of the combination of many of these individual moments together within a conceivable, differentiated chunk, or the Latin *punctum,* translated into English as "point" or "period." From the English translation, it is easy to see that this Latin term could refer to both macro and micro "chunks," and that this word also always refers to the separation of a particular bit from a larger, undifferentiated, even infinite "mass" (the Latin *massa,* or, applied to an aggregated crowd, *turba*). This is exactly the connotation we are after, since we are attempting to understand both the background of, and the rationale behind, a medieval conceptualization of composition and communication.

Let us go on to fill our medieval forest with the "trees" as *materia/substantia* that was known, available, and usable. Augustine—writing two important, though today rather neglected, works at the time of his conversion to Christianity as a young man, around 387—uses both of these concepts. He had journeyed from his home town on the coast of North Africa to study in the center of the Latin-speaking world. In *The Order that Exists Among the Disciplines* (*De ordine*), Augustine discusses what should be learned in school, and the order in which one should attempt to learn subjects, one by one—again the word *order* is a focus for his writing. In both *The Order that Exists Among the Disciplines* and *Concerning Music* (*De musica*), his only work specifically on music, Augustine searches for the secret to music's power, both in education and performance. He finds music's power in the enlivened "body," or particular, limited, enclosed moment of sound, using a "piece" of sound bonded to time and containing vital energy. In *Concerning Music,* he writes that this "piece" of sound is the *pulse,* an enlivened enclosure (or *punctum,* again) of time-sound. In work *The Order that Exists Among the Disciplines,* he argues that since, unlike language, music uses many different sounds, music is much more effective for teaching and learning. The varied and diverse sounds remain in the memory, and, furthermore, the sound of music is delicious to the taste. Sound, therefore, divided into individual tones, and brought together in fitting and appropriate ways, exemplified material substance—an individual, particular "piece" of this substance—and connection or relationship, as these pieces of sound were connected, one after the other, to produce a melody that seemed to make sense. As one traveled—moved on in a sense—from one tone to the next, one was also reminded of the otherwise abstract concept of motion itself. The very nature of motion was exemplified by the process of moving from one piece of sound, or tone, to the next.

Augustine treats *sound* as well as *time,* and the combination of both together, as concrete material to be divided into a separate "body" of the single instant (or pulse). By the same principle, of sound/time as substance, many of these instants could be brought together as a chunk, or, as he states, the contained "body" of the "verse" (*versus*). Notice that the difference is made not between prose and poetry, but between "unlimited" substance and contained, enclosed, enlivened "body."

These otherwise abstract concepts of division and enclosure of sound substance in small, or larger, chunks was specifically applied by this author to music in his treatise on that subject.[6] In fact, Augustine wrote that it was impossible to really understand anything at all unless one understood it through a musical example. Since Augustine was so well-known, wrote so much during his long, productive life, and was taken so seriously, these two concepts of pulse (*pulsus*) and verse (*versus*) provided a foundation for viewing the work of a composer—a "placer-together of chunks"—throughout the period we are discussing, and much later as well. One could argue, even disagree, with Augustine, but one certainly needed to take this author into consideration. We will observe how each major change in how sound was represented in terms of what is called music notation could be related to statements made by Augustine, as well as ways in which he developed seminal concepts within his own writing.

This concept of *chunk*—the self-contained piece of sound substance enclosed, with limitations set from the great, amorphous collection of sound "stuff" here, there, and everywhere—was a concept that, once one was indeed aware of it, and actively looking for it, could be found in many places. One of these was in the *Aeneid* of Virgil, an author Augustine quotes approximately 10,000 times. Augustine knew Virgil, and his epic work that covered, and elaborated upon, Homer's account of the entire fascinating history of how it came to be that the Roman state originated and of what was behind the rise, so to speak, of the city of Rome. Virgil's *Aeneid* was a work that every literate person not only had read but also, to a large extent, knew by heart. Augustine himself appears to have virtually memorized the *Aeneid,* since sometimes he gets it slightly wrong, quoting from the *Aeneid* and incorporating chunks of this epic into his own writing in ways that show that he had internalized, that is, digested and incorporated pieces into his own mentality and writing.[7]

Virgil's *Aeneid* seemed to be made for memorization. The epic is divided into manageable chunks, with titles given by later editors such as "A Fateful Haven," "How They Took the City," "Sea Wanderings and Strange Meetings," "The Passion of the Queen," "Games and Conflagration," "Juno Served by a Fury," "Arcadian Allies," "A Night Sortie, A Day Assault," "The Death of Princes," "Debaters and a Warrior Girl," and "The Fortunes of War." This is a narrative that is divided into "books" or manageable chunks that, in turn, are divided into still more manageable, and memorable, chunks. The famous opening chunks, all of approximately the same size, and each one containing just enough sound material to be read on one breath, gives an example:

> I sing of warfare and a man at war.
> From the sea-coast of Troy in early days
> He came to Italy by destiny,

> To our Lavinian western shore,
> A fugitive, this captain, buffeted
> Cruelly on land as on the sea . . .
> Left by the Greeks and pitiless Achilles,
> Keeping them far from Latium, for years
> They wandered as their destiny drove them on
> From one sea to the next: so hard and huge
> A task it was to found the Roman people.

Every Latin student—from the fourth century, when students, such as Augustine growing up outside of Rome, applied themselves to study Latin as a language that was not their mother tongue, to the late 1960s—eventually memorized:

> Arma virumque cano, Troiae qui primus ab oris
> Italiam fato profugus Laviniaque venit
> litora, multum ille et terris iactatus et alto
> vi superum, saevae memorem Iunonis ob iram,
> multa quoque et bello passus, dum conderet urbem
> inferretque deos Latio; genus unde Latinum
> Albanique patres atque altae moenia Romae,
> Musa, mihi causas memora, quo numine laeso
> quidve dolens regina deum tot voluere casus
> insignem pietate virum, tot adire labores
> impulerit. Tantaene animis caelestibus irae?
> . . . Troas, reliquias Danaum atque immitis Achilli,
> arcebat longe Latio, multosque per annos
> errabant acti fatis maria omnia circum.
> tantae molis erat Romanam condere gentem.[8]

Not only did the lore of how Aeneas left the burning city of Troy to establish a new city—the city of Rome, which he finally accomplished after many dangers, toils, and snares of temptations, enemies on every side, fickle friends and deception, duplicity of every kind, and dirty tricks, as well as utter carnage—capture the imagination of all who could read and understand the Latin language from antiquity to Dante himself in the 14th century; but Virgil's method of construction contained within this powerful, evocative epic was impressed indelibly into the minds not only of Augustine but, again, of all who read and memorized the *Aeneid* from Antiquity to well into the 20th century (see Example I and Example II in chapter IV).

It is remarkable to think of this, how from the first century B.C.E., that is, Virgil's lifetime, through Augustine's, and on, for hundreds of years, the content, vocabulary, and structure of this monumental epic united a mental culture, as well as shaped how people organized and expressed their thoughts. This structure of chunks of material making up the *Aeneid* was a structure that was also visible, not only to the inner eye of the imagination, but to the physical eye as well. The idea of a huge, unlimited stockpile of sounds, concepts, words, piled up and scattered here and there, just waiting for Virgil to come along— or Augustine, or Dante, or even ourselves, in perhaps a more modest enterprise—to "carve out" pieces that could then be fit together into a certain, carefully conceived order for a certain purpose that one had on one's mind, and in one's heart, was a legacy that Virgil gave to the world to come. Many, such as Isidore of Seville, writing in the seventh century C.E., who was read and quoted throughout the Middle Ages, praise him for this, and Christian writers in Late Antiquity, such as a woman by the name of Proba, adapted Virgil's chunks, or *centones*, to use for their own purposes. Everyone, in fact, did this.[9]

The concept of *chunk* was so important because it was not just an abstraction but, rather, was clearly visible to the naked eye, in terms, for example, of the huge building blocks that were left behind in Roman cities here, there, and everywhere all over Europe (see Example III, located at the end of chapter IV). Practically without exception, the cities of Europe were Roman towns—Cologne, London, Vienna, Budapest, to name just a few, and of course, Rome itself. Walls could be seen, and, perhaps, a city-center or forum, and the remains of buildings, the remains of the "Roman day," and the "spoils" (the Latin *spolia*), or leftovers, could be taken by the clever and adventuresome builder to use and reuse for purposes of one's own, taken either by stealth or in broad daylight. This had gone on for centuries, most of all, again, in Rome itself, and it was commonplace to see vast piles of building material around throughout the Roman Empire.[10] Whatever could be carted away and incorporated into another building, for another purpose, was taken away. So we have two powerful visual and visible analogies to the compositional process: chunks of wood within the vast, tangled forest; and piles of blocks within a ruined Roman city. The "worker with materials"—the craftsman, contractor, and composer, working with stones or tones, with words or paints and boards—helped himself and made what he could from what he had at hand and available.

This is true even today, the building material or chunks of material of antiquity—preexistent material—becomes building material to be used right now.)

But there were other sources of the same concept of chunk, or *punctum*, as in its Latin expression, that is, building blocks of many different sizes and shapes, or pieces of wood. One of the most important of these is the Old Testament Book of Psalms, the *Liber psalmorum* as it was known in the Middle Ages. Children who had gone to primary school knew the Book of Psalms by memory, since they learned to read using this book.[11] What, exactly, did their teachers have in mind by this exercise? The psalms, in their variety and diversity, constituted a rich stockpile of figures, of manners or ways of dealing with life, of emotional substance, and of chunks or conceptual building blocks that could be placed as autonomous modules in almost any order. We have, in the Psalms, these varied and diverse *modi*, specifically: (a) the way of thinking or feeling—or mode—of well-being, or the formation of healthful approaches to life and to oneself; (b) a mode in which tempestuous and tumultuous feelings are resolved into tranquility; (c) the mode of "promise" or of future blessings; (d) the mode, also in the future, of judgment; (e) the penitential mode; (f) the mode of forgiveness; (g) the mode of various and diverse letters of the alphabet, or *figurae*, in which each one of the letters externally accesses a hidden, internal force or quality; (h) the mode of death and resurrection; (i) the mode of lamentation, the *deploration*, medieval *planctus*; (j) the mode of repetition of verses in order to impress a meaning upon the mind; (k) the mode of songs that gradually ascend in their emotional state, and as they do this become more and more marvelous, that is, are related to miraculous situations; and finally, (l) the mode of extreme joy.

These modes—or ways of thinking, feeling, acting, and communicating—are found within the rich repository of the 150 psalms, in all of their diversity. They can be seen to be arranged in pairs of contrary modes (or contrary motions), and each one of these modes gave a model, a construct, and an emotional impetus directly and consciously to the musical categories of the Middle Ages—and well beyond this time-frame. The "mode of lamentation" or "deploration," for example, becomes the medieval lamentation or *planctus* in which the author/composer laments the passing away of former joy, or the vanishing through death of a dear friend, as, for example, in the *Planctus of King David*, attributed to the late 12th-century philosophy-teacher-theologian Peter Abelard, as well as 14th-century Machaut's *complaint*. These two examples show how an emotional state found in the Psalms became a recognizable category of composition, and they give evidence for the great influence of the Psalms not only upon daily life of those attending monastic and cathedral schools (of those participating in liturgical events such as the mass and the offices) but also on the daily life of ordinary people. Clearly, the language and compositional categories as well as the emotional levels of the Psalms infiltrated ordinary consciousness and communication. Cassiodorus, commenting on the Psalms in the late fifth century, brings up the "ways of moving" we already observed in "The Enchanted Castle," that is, the mode of taking a situation at face value (the first mode, that of the "institution of health"), of significance for the present; the mode of allegory, or varied and diverse figures that access and stand for a deeply hidden truth; the mode of personal application addressing the question of what one should, under the circumstances, do, or in other words, the "penitential mode" or its opposite, the "praise mode"; and finally, several modes that have to do with the future—of future states, promises, prophesies, and events.

But the Psalms themselves made comprehensible and reinforced the concept of *chunk*. We see this immediately upon opening up the Book of Psalms and reading the first one—a psalm that would most often be marked out in a medieval Psalter with a large, highly decorated, perhaps even illuminated letter *B*:

> Blessed is the man that does not walk in the counsel of the
>   ungodly
> Nor stands in the way of sinners
> Nor sits in the seat of the scornful.
> But his delight is in the law of the Lord
> And in his law he meditates day and night.
> And he shall be like a tree planted by the rivers of water
> That brings forth his fruit in his season
> His leaf also shall not wither
> And whatsoever he does shall prosper.
> The ungodly are not so
> But are as the chaff which the wind drives away.
> Therefore the ungodly shall not stand in the judgment
> Nor sinners in the congregation of the righteous.
> For the Lord knows the way of the righteous
> But the way of the ungodly shall perish.[12]

As shown in Example IV and Example V (in chapter IV), all of these chunks or verses are more or less of the same size, and each one of them has one clear idea—often one that could be translated into one clear image. Each chunk is also just about the size of what can be said in one breath, with a concept that could be retained easily by memory, and delineated by one clear figure. Chunk 1, for example, delineates the figure of "the man" who is happy or "blessed." Secondly, the chunks occur in contrast pairs, or as statement, counterstatement. Another way of describing this method of communication would be that the second chunk either reinforces the first or directly contrasts with it, and so it goes through the entire psalm. (One could express this method by using the phrase "on the one hand" contrasted by the phrase "on the other hand," and this usage is obviously an effective, much-used way of communicating in teaching, preaching, political speech-making, and even in ordinary conversation. One can use this method of construction with parallel pairs in almost every situation.) The Book of Psalms is a quarry, so to speak, of chunks with figures designating each chunk, with a contrast made often between the single figure, that is, "Blessed is *the man*" (*Beatus vir*). The "man" is the subject of both the beginning psalm of the Psalter, psalm 1, as well as psalm 112: "Blessed is the man that feareth the Lord, that delights greatly in his commandments." The single "blessed man" contrasts with many figures "Blessed are *they*" (*Beati immaculati*), the opening line of Psalm 119. What seems to be important in the psalms is just this contrast between the single *figura* and the plurality of varied and diverse figures that, in all their variety and diverse qualities and attributes, together constitute an "alphabet" of figures (*figurae*) doing many different things, for many different reasons, each with a distinctive gesture.

The entire resource of the Book of Psalms is made up of these chunks. All of these chunks were taken apart, as building blocks, or as imaginary logs within a forest, and put back together again. To this day, we do not know who was responsible for this, whether a group of composers—the word "composer" literally means a person who "places together"—or a single person. Some, in the ninth century and later, thought that the sixth-century pope Gregory the Great was single-handedly responsible for this feat.[13] But whoever did it, and for whatever reason, the result of this deconstruction and recombination of the Book of Psalms was that sound material was united with communication in different and arresting ways. Instead of the complete psalm, known in its entirety, and in a certain order, by memory, the chunks of a given psalm, such as the one cited above, were disengaged from one another, placed together in new ways, so that component parts of a psalm could be spread out among many different compositions throughout the entire year of singing, day in and day out. An analogous situation would be if all of the sections of "Fiordinando" were pried apart and recombined in many entirely different contexts.[14]

Furthermore, the figure of "the Blessed Man" (*Beatus vir*) also served as a marker for an entire passage, or extended chunk, a *versus*. In a sense, this figure traveled here and there, reappearing in various contexts, as the following three examples show. The concept of the single figure, "The Happy Man," turns up, so to speak, in one place as a gradual, in another as an alleluia verse, and still another as a tract, all entities within the ordered time of the Mass ceremony, as well as places within equally ordered times of the year. In still another context, "the Happy Man" is featured as a complete psalm. The figure of "the Happy Man," then, is a traveler, from one place in time to another.

This is the way it worked. The chunks of Psalm 112, beginning with the concept of the single figure ("Blessed is the man who fears the Lord," *Beatus vir qui timet Dominum*), have been separated, in the following examples, both from their order within the Psalms—an order that everyone would have known very well indeed—and taken from the remaining chunks of psalm 112. One must keep in mind that the entire psalm with its succession of verses would have been well known by all who sang it, whether or not they could read and write. Separation into chunks throughout highlighted individual *figurae*, such as "the Happy Man," drew attention to both structure and content, since those who knew it well were not proceeding more or less automatically, by repetition, but rather, by a new lack of familiarity, they were forced to think about the new order of chunks. Further, even if one makes no attempt to actually read the musical *figurae* or notation, it is plain to see that the same words are placed together with quite different musical tones, and it is also clear that there are long stretches of tones alone—no text at all, as in the gradual, over *Dominum* (the Lord), or after *terra* (earth), or after *benedicetur* (will be blessed). So the concept of chunk was applied on more than one level, including musical sound all by itself. Here are the chunks of the psalm (verses 1–2):

> *Beatus vir, qui timet Dominum*
> (Blessed is the man who fears the Lord)
> *in mandatis ejus cupit nimis.*
> (Takes delight in his commandments)
>
> (*versus*)
>
> *Potens in terra erit semen eius*
> (Powerful on the earth will be his seed)
> *Generatio rectorum benedicetur.*
> (The generation of the righteous will be blessed.)

We find the concept of *Beatus vir* in several categories of chant, or *cantus,* as we see from Examples VI, VII, and VIII, in chapter IV.

Compare all three of these examples with the chunks of the complete psalm, as given, and you will see that the first two verses used by the gradual, alleluia, and tract are extracted from the complete psalm. What would have followed these three pieces within the Mass ceremony would have been chunks taken from many other contexts, like building blocks taken from their former locations and put in new locations for new reasons.

The Book of Psalms served as a great repository, a mighty and vast source of possibilities, movements, figures, both of sign and of thought, or contrary positions and reactions resolved into concord of emotions. The Book of Psalms was, for medieval composers and commentators, a forest that was opaque with tangled branches, a welter, even clutter of resources. And everyone helped themselves; each person who interacted with the *cantus,* as well as those now anonymous abbots, teachers, commentators[15] who broke apart the building blocks of the Psalms and placed them together again within medieval *cantus,* including many others through the centuries, such as Augustine, Hildegard of Bingen, and Peter Abelard (11th–12th centuries), helped themselves to its phrases, language, expressions, and emotional substance.[16] The "material" of the Psalms, in chunks, was available to all, and each helped him or herself, according to purpose and mastery. The "order" (*ordo*) of the Psalms, too, could be worked with, with chunks taken out of context and repositioned to enhance a topic and make a point. The psalms, loaded as they were with communicational possibilities, were available to be joined to other sound material—distinct musical tones. This "joining" of the psalms to music tones, and the use of the Book of Psalms as a repository for topics, vocabulary, and ways of articulating emotional substance has taken place to the present day. One need only to reflect for a few minutes on the use of the Book of Psalms, or portions—chunks—of the individual psalms within music composition of the 20th century: for example, Stravinsky's *Symphony of Psalms.*

NOTES

1. We will use the Latin expressions *substantia / materia* rather than the more familiar "matter," with its much later connotations of "materialism," for which the distinction between "seen" material and the unseen, or "spiritual," is pivotal. This medieval equivalence between seen and unseen *materia / substancia* will come up again and again.

2. See *Cicero Refused to Die: Ciceronian Influence Through the Centuries,* ed. Nancy van Deusen (in press) for the impact of Cicero, both as a consciously crafted *persona* as well as his writings, especially within medieval education.

3. Cicero, *The Nature of Gods* (*De natura deorum*), edited with English translation by H. Rackham, Loeb Classical Library, *Cicero Collected Works,* vol. 19, (Cambridge, MA, 1933; repr. 1994]); Cicero's discussion of Homer and other writers, i.41; ii.70,165; iii.11,41; various touches, odors, sounds, i.112–113; "occasion" as an enclosed interval or body of time-substance, in *Concerning*

Invention (*De inventione*), ed., trans. by H.M. Hubbell, Loeb Classical Library, Cicero Collected Works, vol. 2 (Cambridge, MA, 1949; repr. 1963), i.vi.8–9; i.xxvi.39ff. Cicero writes of the "material" of which speeches are made, that is "rhetorical material." One can deal with this material in terms of what is said (*dixerunt*); what is made of this material or drawn out of it (*inventio*); how one disposes it (*dispositio*); how it is amplified it (*elocutio*); or how it is stored away in the memory (*memoria*); and, interestingly, the conscious shaping that is done with this sound material as one pronounces words (*pronuntiatio*). It is as if one had all of the sound to be used everywhere at one's disposal, and one selected portions of it in order to shape and "dispose" of it. Cicero goes on to enlarge upon his concept of a limited "part" of sound, as well as a "part" of time, that is, an *occasion* as a "space of time."

   4. H.M. Hubbell, ed., trans. *Concerning Invention* (*De inventione*) Loeb Classical Library, Cicero Collected Works, vol. 2 (Cambridge, MA, 1949; repr. 1963), i, xxvi, 39.

   5. Quintilian, *The Institutio Oratoria of Quintilian,* 4 vols., ed., trans. H.E. Butler, Loeb Classical Library (Cambridge, MA, 1920; repr. 1958), X.iii.17–18, especially:

> Diversum est huic eorum vitium, qui primo decurrere *per materiam* stilo quam velocissimo volunt et sequentes calorem atque impetum ex tempore scribunt; *hanc silvam* vocant. Repetunt deinde et componunt quae effuderant; sed verba emendantur et numeri, manet in rebus temere congestis quae fuit levitas. Protinus ergo adhibere curam rectius erit atque ab initio sic opus ducere, ut caelandum non ex integro fabricandum sit. Aliquando tamen adfectus sequemur, in quibus fere plus calor quam diligentia valet. (Emphasis added.)

Per materiam, ex tempore, silvam, componunt, congestis, sic opus ducere, ex integro fabricandum sit are expressions used frequently, and they all have specific significance. The Latin quotation has been included here for the following reason. This passage not only contains good advice, no doubt one of the reasons why Quintilian continued to be read for such a long time; it is also indicative of a common translational error in which specific Latin terms with a long background of usage are obscured or even completely left out by the English translation. The Latin text has been translated:

> On the other hand, there is a fault which is precisely the opposite of this, into which those fall who insist on first making a rapid draft of their subject with the utmost speed of which their pen is capable, and write in the heat and impulse of the moment. *They call this their rough copy.* They then revise what they have written, and arrange their hasty outpourings. But while the words and the rhythm may be corrected, the matter is still marked by the superficiality resulting from the speed with which it was thrown together. The more correct method is, therefore, to exercise care from the very beginning, and to form the work from the outset in such a manner that it merely requires to be chiseled into shape, and not fashioned anew. (Emphasis added.)

Note here the use of the word *silva,* as well as *congestis* in the Latin text, as inchoate *materia*; the translator did not understand why *silva* was used in this context, and his translation, therefore, neglects to bring it out. This example shows how translations can obscure, even cover up, important terms and their meanings.

6. It is interesting to observe what Augustine delineated under the topic of music. Rather than melody, Augustine deals with the concept of the enlivened "chunk" or delimited, contained "body" of the pulse, and various patterns of recurring pulses together within the "body" of the *versus*.

7. For Augustine's allusions to, uses of, and incorporation of both the concept of chunks as well as actually pieces of Virgil's writing into his own thought and works, see Sabine MacCormack, *The Shadows of Poetry: Vergil in the Mind of Augustine* (Berkeley-Los Angeles, 1998); cf. her preface, pp. xviif:

> Vergil and Augustine are very different authorial personalities. Vergil wrote slowly, with much revising, and the volume of all his poems will fit into a small purse. Augustine, by contrast, usually wrote rather quickly and his works take up several feet on the shelves of a library. But the two share one characteristic: they both wrote for their contemporaries at large, not merely for the erudite few, and they wrote about topics that captured the imagination . . . Vergil has been understood differently in different historical periods and by different people. Some readers, most notably Dante in the early fourteenth century, followed by numerous scholars of our own time, have discovered in Vergil a validation and even a eulogy of the Roman Empire, others have discovered the very opposite. It is not the case that evidence and arguments justifying such divergent interpretations cannot be found in Vergil's text . . . In some instances, Augustine quoted from Vergil as part of a thought or a line of reasoning, referring to the famous poet in order to help convince his readers. At other times, however, he cited lines or half-lines of Vergil quite informally as part of his own mental furniture. Put differently, Vergil formed part of the very shape of Augustine's reality because he described reality in ways that Augustine found decisive.

This passage has been quoted in full because it succinctly makes the case for the influence of Virgil not only upon Augustine, but during the entire period under discussion, that is, to the 14th century.

8. *P. Vergili Maronis Opera*, ed. R.A.B. Mynors (Oxford, 1969), pp. 103–104. Compare the shifting accentual patterns with editions of the sequence given in Edition IV.

9. Cf, Isidore of Seville, *Origines* I, 39 (38) *De Hist. Scriptoribus Eccles.* Cap. 5:

> *Proba, uxor Adelphii proconsulis, femina inter viros ecclesiasticos idcirco posita sola, pro eo quod in laude Christi versata est, componens centonem de Christo Virgilianis coaptatum versiculis. Cuius quidem non miramur studium, sed laudamus ingenium. Quod tamen opusculum legitur inter apocryphas Scripturas insertum.*
>
> Proba, the wife of Alphus the proconsul, a woman amongst male churchmen, is to be praised. For her adaptation of Virgil's *versiculi* is not so much a wonder of scholarship, but of ingenuity.

See also van Deusen, *Theology and Music*, p. 132. Proba's work has been edited, *Centonum poetria*, in *Patrologiae latinae cursus completus* . . . series *Latina*, ed. J-P Migne, 218 vols. (Paris, 1879–1890), XIV.802–816.

10. In fact, the word *commonplace* signifies just that, a self-contained chunk of thought that is already there, with which to begin a discussion, or as a capstone to end it. Commonplace is the Greek *topos*, the Latin *locus topici*, a topic to be used. This is an important term and concept in the Middle Ages, certainly still with us today, not only in the English translation, but other languages as

well, such as the German *Gemeinplätze*. Commonplaces or *topoi* are discussed by Cicero, Quintilian, Augustine, Boethius, and Aristotle, and it is interesting to observe subtle shifts of meaning and understanding of this concept throughout the Middle Ages. Here, we draw attention to the concrete implications of a term that refers to conceptual *substantia* as it can be found in a manageable, recognizable, self-contained block or chunk. Examples of such *topoi* might be: "education is important for children," "the State needs to manage its money wisely," " those who do well should be rewarded," etc.—more or less what are considered to be dispositive and apparent truths that require no further explanation. (See Quintilian, *Institutio* II.i.1,9,11; IV.vii.4; V.i.3; V.xiii.57; X.v.12; XI.i.46. Quintilian, referring to Cicero, asks: Are not commonplaces at the very heart of lawsuits? They make a great impression on judges. But sometimes what seems to be most apparent can be false.)

11. See George H. Brown, "The Psalms as the Foundation of Anglo-Saxon Learning" and Joseph Dyer, "The Psalms in Monastic Prayer," in *The Place of the Psalms in the Intellectual Culture of the Middle Ages*, ed. Nancy van Deusen (Binghamton, NY, 1999), pp. 1–17, 53–83.

12. For comparison, see the Latin Vulgate (it is also of interest to compare the following with the many variants within medieval Psalters):

> Beatus vir qui non abiit in consilio impiorum, Et in via peccatorum non stetit, Et in cathedra pestilentiae non sedit; Sed in lege Domini voluntas eius, Et in lege eius meditabitur die ac nocte. Et erit tanquam lignum quod plantatum est secus decursus aquarum, Quod fructum suum dabit in tempore suo: Et folium eius non defluet; Et omnia quaecumque faciet prosperabuntur. Non sic impii, non sic; Sed tanquam pulvis quem proiicit ventus a facie terrae. Ideo non resurgent impii in iudicio, Neque peccatores in concilio iustorum, Quoniam novi Dominus viam iustorum: Et iter impiorum peribit.

> *Quoted from the Biblia sacra iuxta vulgatam clementinam, nova editio,*
> *Alberto Colunga, OP, Laurentio Turrado, eds. (Madrid, 1977).*

13. Paul the Deacon, a Lombard, writing in the ninth century attributes the composition of the entire graduale or book containing all of the *cantus* (texts and music) for the entire year, that is, the temporale dealing with the events during Christ's life such as Advent, Nativity, and Easter, and portions of the sanctorale, or celebrations of certain saints, to Pope Gregory the Great. But there are more than three centuries between the death of Pope Gregory and the appearance of music notation in many parts of Europe; and there is otherwise no indication in terms of evidence for inclination, talent, or actual activity of this kind on the part of this Pope. Medieval biographers must be considered one by one as to purpose and agenda, as well as authorial personality. To add more confusion, there are two "Paul the Deacons." One, writing ca. 780, a biographer of Chrodegang and the bishops of Metz, gives credit to Chrodegang for undertaking sweeping reforms and revising the *cantus* on the advice of Rome; the other Paul the Deacon, mentioned at the beginning of this note, was an historian of the Lombards who also wrote a far-reaching biography of Pope Gregory the Great. Concerning the attention to be paid to them, as well as the evaluation of the kind of witness they offer, the Paul the Deacon who

is the biographer of Chrodegang is the only source for the *cantus*-reforming activities of Bishop Chrodegang, and the Bishop's understandable interest in the liturgy of Rome should not be taken to necessarily include specific text-music situations (namely, *cantus*). Further, Paul the Deacon should also be placed within the context that one does not, as Claussen points out, even know when Bishop Chrodegang was born, nor is there consensus concerning the spelling of his name. Nevertheless, both Pauls have had amazing influence and have been repeatedly quoted, and their statements have been the bases of entire hypothetical structures concerning the Gregorian chant, as well as so-called Old-Roman chant. The crucial point here is that, regardless of who wrote what, the earliest *figurae* of music notation are from the late 9th, early 10th century. It is perhaps a lack of seriousness based on misunderstanding of the place and role of music as a medieval discipline that has influenced writers in the 20th century to quote with unreflective trust the sparse statements, only possibly concerning music, based on, in these cases, only two sources. For the eighth-century Paul the Deacon, see M. A. Claussen, *The Reform of the Frankish Church. Chrodegang of Metz and the regula canonicorum in the Eighth Century* (Cambridge, UK, 2004).

14. Italo Calvino, *If on a Winter's Day a Traveler,* trans. William Weaver (New York, 1979); and *The Castle of Crossed Destinies,* trans. William Weaver (New York, 1977): both rely upon self-contained modules or chunks that can be placed in almost any order.

15. There is a similar, contemporaneous problem with the complete commentary on all of the books of the Old and New Testaments, eventually to become the so-called *glossa ordinaria.* Nearly all of the earlier commentators remain without sure identification, although names such as Berengar of Tours, a certain Drogo, Haimo and Heiric of Auxerre, Remigius of Auxerre, Haimo of Halberstadt, Paschasius Radbertus, Rhabanus Maurus, Walafrid Strabo, and Anselm of Laon all come down to us as reasonable suspects. Beryl Smalley noted that even in the 9th and 10th centuries, commentators themselves were probably unsure of exactly who wrote individual commentaries. The *glossa ordinaria* was revised, came to a more or less complete state in the 11th and 12th centuries, and continued to be emended and expanded upon well into the 12th century with commentators such as Peter Comester and Peter Lombard. It is perhaps a sign of the trivialization of music that although *cantus* has been attributed to "improvisation," implying a traditional, or more or less serendipitous, compositional method, this has never been the case for the *glossa ordinaria.* Perhaps, given the place of music within an entertainment culture today, words are, generally speaking, treated with greater seriousness than music, or even words *with* music as is the case for *cantus.* Yet, it must be kept in mind, syllables bonded to music tones within *cantus* were taken from the biblical scriptures—most commonly, the Psalms; and some commentators, such as Remigius of Auxerre, who wrote on music as an analogical discipline also wrote commentaries on the Psalms. There is, therefore, a close, even co-terminus, position of syllable with tone, in that tone in a sense partakes of syllable and vice versa. Further, as will be seen in examples below, one of the goals of the "fashioners" of *cantus* was apparently to conceptualize

a text-music situation in which neither text nor tone would dominate, but, rather, each would serve to transmit the other. The fashioners of *cantus* succeeded in a remarkable way. See also Beryl Smalley, "Monastic and Cathedral Schools," in *The Study of the Bible in the Middle Ages*, pp. 37–82, especially pp. 56, 62–66.

16. For the infiltration of the language of the Psalms into communication of many kinds, see especially Michael P. Kuczynski, "The Psalms and Social Action in Late Medieval England," in *The Place of the Psalms in the Intellectual Culture of the Middle Ages*, pp. 173–195.

4

Music within the Context of Medieval Education

In this chapter, we return to "Fiordinando," where we found the issue of material substance that is unlimited and disorderly as it is found in the world (preexistent substance), blocks or chunks of this material, as well as the idea of separating portions of an otherwise chaotic substance (*cento = punctum*), the concept of order itself (*ordo*), and the union or "marriage" between substance and its communication (*figura,* varied and diverse *figurae, copula*), as well as the ways or manners in which this communication can take place (*modus, modi*). In this investigation, what is interesting—even amazing—is that there is, in a sense, no cleft between learning and engaged amusement; as well as no separation between education and experience. All of these attributes that make up a composition were to be found in an amusing story, and could, with some reflection, be applied as well to incidents one might encounter in real-life experience. As the result of one's own engagement with the story, one could select—pick out—and reflect on the details of "Fiordinando" in order to apply them to one's own time, place, and individual, recognizable circumstances, and, in fact, this process is exactly what makes the story worth reading. In other words, what we have here is not on the one hand "school" and on the other "story" but rather a story that makes sense, yet is, along the way, making one point after the other. One is also given, almost surreptitiously, an entire toolbox full of tools—tools for thinking, for analyzing, and for expressing oneself. These tools also have to do with materials, their specific properties, how to measure them, as well as how to speak of them.

What tools do we have in mind, and how can these tools be applied, not only to reading and understanding "Fiordinando" but also to understanding the larger issues of communication and artistic work—that is, work that is carefully considered, the result of materials selected and dealt with—as developed in the Middle Ages? We are also bringing together individual elements that constitute what has been called a medieval "mentality"—those priorities and concepts as well as educational experiences that medieval intellectual culture shared and transmitted, sometimes in subtle ways, to the present. We find, first of all, the notion of *particular* things. We meet early on, particular people, particular figures with particular qualities about them that make them recognizable, so that when they appear again, we can identify them and postulate a reason for their reappearance. A king, a prince, a queen, a hunter, a monster, an innkeeper, a hermit—all of them are single figures—delineatory outlines—yet all together they present a spectrum of varied and diverse figures. We can see them before us with the eye of the imagination; but the same principle can be made clear within the two subjects that discuss particulars, namely the study of grammar as a communicational field, discussing both single letters or figures, as well as all of the letters of the alphabet, or varied and diverse figures. The parallel material discipline is arithmetic that, in terms of material substance, discusses measurement in terms of single numbers, such as the number (or *figura*) one or two, and so on. So, we see a marriage coming to pass between communication and material in terms of particularity as this concept is presented as letters of the alphabet, or exemplified by numbers that refer, most often, to a visible, measurable thing. On the one hand, particularity is expressed by *sound*; on the other hand, particularity is *measured*.[1]

To continue: in "Fiordinando," relationships are of the utmost importance. In fact, without connections, there would be no story at all. We noticed, first of all, the connection between the king and the prince, then the prince and the hunter, the prince and his mother, and so on, until this connection broke down. Every one of the connections are based on physical presence as well as exchanged dialogue—people speak to one another, and confront one another. Their faces are turned toward one another. Not so with the "Queen of Portugal," whose face is veiled, and her lips are sealed, so that, in spite of the fact that her material physical presence is in the room of the palace, it is impossible for the other characters to really made connection with her—either by eye contact or by verbal exchange. The breakdown in communicational connection made the point of the connection that much more drastic.

This specific example could lead to the study of connection or relationship in general. One of the reasons why we are able to make sense of the story is that there is also a logical connection, to a certain extent, between the chunks as they occur one by one. The study of logic gave a medieval reader tools to describe how this was, or could be the case, and focused upon connection within written and spoken communication. To explain and delineate what it was that one had in mind, one could use figures, both figures of speech and figures of thought (*sche-mata*, as Quintilian and Cassiodorus classified them),[2] such as comparisons, analogies, and metaphors. Medieval logic's parallel study dealt with connection as it occurs in, and can be exemplified by, geometry, a study that also dealt with very practical and clearly substantial matters, such as the measuring and surveying of plots of land, and determining whether one's neighbor had built a fence on one's own property or not. Connection, both as an abstraction and as a practical reality, was plain to see in terms of connected lines within geometric figures (again the word *figure*) and in the practical reality of pieces of land, in which, of course, a miscalculation or the absence of correct connection could end up in a court of law. So, again, communication and material were united in terms of two disciplines that dealt with a common project, that is, relationship, on the one hand, as communication or logic; and, on the other, as material and measurement within geometry. And again, one learned both by means of figures, both singly and in terms of varied and diverse figures, word and thought *figurae* in logic, and triangles or heptagons in geometry.

In "Fiordinando," if there was one thing to be noted, it is motion, as well as diverse qualities of motion, more or less constantly throughout the story. (This sense of forward thrust or ongoing motion is enhanced by the sentences that move forward with punctuation but only rarely with complete breaks.) The prince rides out into the forest, rides further and further into the forest, rides back home, rides back into the forest, rides into the thickest part of the forest, rides back home, rides to Paris, and rides to St. Petersburg, where he participates in a tournament, jousting each day. We are continually confronted with motion. We are also brought into contact with the motion that is set up by communication: the motion of thought and word, so to speak, as both are exchanged between the varied and diverse figures that mark out the plot. These figures make the plot move along, and as readers we are caught up in this motion from one event to the next. Again, the concept of figure, both as a single figure, as well as varied and diverse figures, is essential for the movement of the story, the movement of discussion among the figures, and, especially, the physical movement of imagined bodies moving from place to place. That movement itself is much more important than the realistic measurement of distance, and mode of transportation, is seen by the fact that no mention is made in the story of the long, overland, ride by carriage from Paris to St. Petersburg. The nature of motion is obviously more at stake here than precise details or attributes of this motion.

"Fiordinando," again, presents for our view a pair of disciplines that give us tools for understanding what motion is all about. The first of these is communicational, teaching, and bringing to the attention of all, ways or modes of speaking and writing so that effective motion is set up, and an audience is convinced and energized, rather than sent off to sleep. Internal motions, or *emotions,* are aroused so that actions are effected and feelings are affected.[3] This, in a nutshell, is the science or discipline of rhetoric, and those who communicate effectively or move the emotions of crowds are rhetoricians. Rhetoric, as Quintilian in his four books of rhetoric discussed thoroughly, depends upon the use of figures to make points—figures such as metaphor and analogy, but also example, ridicule, and irony, either one at a time, or as varied and diverse figures.[4] All are effective, and Quintilian listed them one by one, as there are many of them.

Rhetoric's parallel discipline that also deals with movement, but in terms of material and measurement, is the science of moving physical bodies, or astronomy, followed by physics. Figures are also of much importance for this science, as astronomers link stars into constellations and find figures in order to recognize and describe "The Big Dipper" or "Orion" and "Cassiopeia"; and—especially after the translation into Latin, and widespread discussion of Aristotle's *Physics* in the late 12th and early 13th centuries—the nature, trajectory, containment, and course of movement.

This, then, is an orderly, rational, and complete system for studying basic principles of reality, such as particulars, connections, and movement in pairs, thus bringing the communication necessary for teaching and learning together with the physical realities and certainties of numbers, connected lines that could delineate plots of ground, and physical motion. What we have described was current as a system of education that combined mental tools—dealing with written letters, numbers, diagrams, and drawings, all of which would have been united within the Latin word *figura*—with life itself, as it could be observed. Augustine describes this system in "The Order that Exists Among the Disciplines."[5] Chalcidius also describes this system in his commentary on Plato's *Timaeus.* This system of parallel disciplines was, in turn, a foundation and background for thinking, teaching, and learning from the beginning of the 9th century to the 14th. In fact, what we have described would have been recognizable well into the 20th century. In other words, a lack of familiarity with this system of related disciplines, as well as the structure that made them comprehensible and useful, is very recent indeed.

Augustine presented areas of study in an order to be studied,[6] beginning with certainties that children could easily master, including: letters as figures (*figurae*) that indicated and delineated sound; numbers indicating particular things; the study of logic with the study of connected thoughts; the connected lines of geometricized material; and the study of motions, both in communication and to be observed in the heavens. These areas of study were to be undertaken with one purpose in mind, that is, having first discovered ways of dealing with things seen and heard, such as objects and sound, and in finding out manners of drawing these things to others' attention in terms of communication. One might go on to study to things unseen that were also impossible to be heard: Augustine was thinking expressly of God and how one, through the physical universe that involved the senses, might come to ways or manners of dealing with what could not be perceived with the senses, but that was, nevertheless, substantial. He was certainly not alone in this project, since both Plato and Aristotle were concerned with the same process and progress toward unseen substance. This was, for Plato, soul. For Aristotle, this unseen substance could be designated as "soulish substance," or "life itself" contained within "ensouled bodies." For Aristotle, "containment" was an issue, not the soulish substance itself.[7] The works of both of these authors were increasingly available to a Latin (not only Greek) reading public during the course of the Middle Ages. As we have mentioned, some of Plato's *Timaeus,* with an extensive commentary, was translated by Chalcidius in the late third or early fourth century C.E. to be followed by translations of the *Phaedo* and the *Meno* by a Sicilian, Henricus Aristippus, in the 1150s. Some of Aristotle's logical works, such as the *Topics* and *Prior Analytics,* were translated by Boethius (known throughout the Middle Ages as the "Old Logic," *logica vetus*), and many of Aristotle's most important works, such as the *Physics, Metaphysics, Poetics,* the *Ethics,* the *Posterior Analytics,* and his treatise concerning the soul and soulish substance (*Concerning the Soul, De anima*), were translated in the late 12th century and on through the 13th century. The translations caused a great stir and provided a foundation of discussion for commentators for at least the next 300 years.[8]

We will leave aside an unresolved question of how much either Plato's or Aristotle's works, especially on the soul, Augustine knew well, or the more general question of his mastery of the Greek language so that he could have read these authors, and others, in the original language; instead, we take up a topic that is more to the point here. All three of these authors, Plato, Aristotle, and Augustine, who were of such enormous, indeed incalculable, influence throughout the period known as the Middle Ages, had a common persuasion, namely, that music constituted, and indeed fashioned, a bridge between communication and material and measurement—between the communicational disciplines and those that dealt with "stuff"—and the unseen, but also very real "stuff" of life itself, or "soulish substance." Music stands, then, between "voice" and "stuff," between expression and the substance of this expression, or between articulation and content. In other words, music is the halfway house between what one says and what one knows: music combines both what is said and known and makes both present in an immediate sensation.

In the Middle Ages, music, by using the unseen substances of time, sound, and motion, exemplified *life* as an unseen, nevertheless, utterly motivational force. For this reason music was studied in medieval education and was continued to be regarded as the "analogy discipline" to be studied by every school child, right on to university training as was formulated in the 13th century, first in Paris, Oxford, and all over the continent of Europe, with disciplines continuing the program already established by Augustine, but with new intellectual impetus and tools provided by the recent translations of Aristotle, particularly the *Physics* and the *Metaphysics*. There was also a new disciplinary force for unification and understanding in that Aristotle presented intellectual tools in the *Metaphysics* that were in turn exemplified in specific ways through a particular disciplinary window in the *Physics*, the *Poetics*, as well as the *Ethics*.[9] What was clear to Plato and Aristotle, according to the examples they include, and later to Augustine, was the fact that music discloses realities that can otherwise be understood with great difficulty, or not at all. "Nothing can be understood, except through music," wrote Augustine in the fourth century C.E., and it seemed that the rest of the Middle Ages was, at least in part, devoted to coming to terms with and actually implementing what Augustine meant by this. During the middle years of the 13th century, Roger Bacon, then a professor at the University of Paris, was still puzzling over, but agreeing with, Augustine on this score. "Trust me on this," is what Augustine seems to be saying.[10]

Let us review these fields of learning, their relationship to one another, and the notion of music as an "Exemplification Discipline." All of these disciplines use *figurae* as an indicative, delineational means of establishing differentiation and identity within *ways* of movement and understanding (or *modes*) as we see here:

grammar *figura*:   a, b, c, etc.

logic *figura*:   (connected *figurae* or *figurae* within syntax that shows logical connection)

rhetoric *figura*:   metaphor (one example of "figure of thought" in which one word is understood but with another meaning, in order to "move" the mind and emotions, that is to persuade [turn around, or *translatio*]), pleonasm, metonymy, etc.

arithmetic *figura*:   1, 2, 3, etc. (change from Roman to Arabic *figurae*, early 14th century).
geometry *figura*:   triangle, circle, square, etc.
physics *figura*:   Orion, Taurus, Pleiades, etc.
music *figura*:   *virga punctum*

All of these disciplines are intrinsically unified by the term *figura* since *figura* is common to all of them, as seen above. This is an instantaneous unification that could easily escape notice today, since a different word for each is used within the English language, as, for example, letter, sentence, metaphor, number, triangle, constellation, music notation, showing how important connections made in the Middle Ages, within the Latin language, are no longer available in English translation. This, perhaps, is a definition, in a nutshell, of cultural difference, whether of time, or geographical region, namely, that one culture separates what another brings together into one unified, connected, informational field. Connections intrinsic to one culture are not always made in another.

As a matter of fact, *figurae* as delineating individuals, relationships, and movement appear to meet us nearly everywhere in the Middle Ages. Here we have examples from an important manuscript of the 10th and 11th centuries, as in Figure 4.9, now in the Latin manuscript collection of the National Library in Paris.

These figures by their gestures, visages, clothing, hand positions, and instruments indicate and communicate ways of moving and understanding (modes). The series begins, as in "Fiordinando," with the "kingly figure." Throughout the series, motion is accentuated by means of the *figurae* of music instruments, colors, and gestures, all coming together in the last of this series, in which dance, as *figurae in modis,* comes to the fore. The *figurae* appear to contain and to communicate as well, internal, *emotional* motion, in terms of facial expressions, limp, hanging hands (or, more obviously, red hands), and, again, instruments. It is important to keep in mind that instruments were also designated as *figurae* in the Middle Ages. All of these illustrations, either singly in their individuality, each as a single *figura,* as well as all together as "varied and diverse figures," or *charactere variarae* (*charivari*), illustrate the points we have been considering. A further observation could be made here. These illustrations break down separations that one might be taken for granted today such as the division between "sacred" and "secular," playfulness and seriousness, study and activity. A separation between texts written in the Latin language, compared to emerging vernacular or, increasingly, spoken languages, such as Anglo-Saxon in England (before the 11th-century Norman conquest), Anglo-Norman, Middle French, medieval German, can be found, and a difference made between "vernacular," and "Latin" languages, but not between categories of "sacred" and "secular" as may be perceived today. We will return to this topic later, since it focuses upon such an important cultural difference between recognized and acceptable contemporary views, the cultures under discussion here, and music within the intellectual culture of the Middle Ages.

In Figure 4.10, *figurae* in various modes of expression and communication are included, side by side, as text alone, music and text together, and drawings. *Figurae* are everywhere in this "Romance" even the name "FAUVEL," in which each letter or *figura* of the name delineates a property, with all of them together, one by one in a logical order, giving forth relationship—a work that demonstrates how comprehensive and influential the mental background especially concerning the term, *figura*, under discussion here remained, in this case, at least into the 14th century.

This is a shift from ways in which music is often regarded today. Rather then providing a pleasant diversion after a hard day at school or work; reassurance for weary travelers in a huge and hectic airport; a soothing, relaxing ambiance for eating and drinking with friends in a restaurant; or a presence in an empty house for those who live alone, music for medieval people made difficult things plain and opened their eyes to understanding the complex secrets of the universe. Music pried open the hard shell that covered truth. No other field of learning shared this distinction, and no one really challenged this capacity of music to make principles of particularity, individuality, connection, and motivation plain. Only well after the 14th century did it occur to anyone to argue that because drawing exemplified life more directly with its figures and shapes, it should stand in the place of music as an analogical discipline, did music have any competition as an exemplary discipline.[11]

What did music make plain, and how, exactly, did music accomplish this task? Let us take a look at these medieval exemplifications, both for the principles they illustrate, as well as for themselves as music, and, at the same time, as expressions of the cultures and the people that made them.

First of all, let us return to the Latin word *silva*, which, we have seen, signified, for many hundreds of years, a boundless, unlimited, disorderly thicket—a true *forest* or repository of material. If the purpose at hand is to separate manageable twigs from this forest, then the medieval music notational figure does exactly this. The two *figurae* of music notation are the *virga* (twig) and the *punctum* (an enclosed piece of material); and upon these two separations of individual bits from the forest of possible material substance, *cantus* is given discretion and individual delineation by means of combinations of these two *figurae*.

But day in and day out, music was actually sung and also played. Each time this happened—for example, in churches, courts, and schools—by the very nature of music and language as using sound substance, a coalition—a conspiracy—was set up between the *figurae* of letters in the texts that were at the same time sung, together with the *figurae* of music notation. This coalition was especially meaningful to those who actually did the singing, since one learned by doing and experiencing, even by, as medieval authors state, *tasting* the tone in one's mouth. Each day, every day, the principle of *particularity* in terms of tone, as well as individual sounds (for example, the vowel *e* in the Latin word, *tecum*), as well as the *connection* between the letters that followed, one after the other, and the tones that did exactly the same thing, made both particularity and connection abundantly plain. Furthermore, as one moved from one letter and tone to the next, one experienced *motion,* in the same way as one experiences food when one eats it. Everyone *sang* particularity, relationship, and motion. All participants who sang experienced these basic principles, as they became increasingly acquainted with them day by day as children in schools. In a sense, it was the best education possible, since it combined knowledge with experience, showing how, ultimately, what one knew needed to be both communicated and put into action in order to be truly understood. We see this in the following lengthy example, which gives the events, one after the other, of an important day. Each portion of the day is marked out by conceptual figure, as one can see:

Let us move through an edition and English translation of the service of Epiphany taken from an early 12th-century manuscript, also in the National Library of Paris, from Nevers Cathedral in middle France. The edition brings out an entire day's program, beginning, in this case, with the night before, and the evening section, and continuing throughout the next day. This service also tells us something about a special geographical situation, since it took place in a cathedral. The celebration deals with Epiphany, celebrated simultaneously as the Feast of the Church; Christ's baptism by John the Baptist; the appearance of the Magi, or the Three Kings; and the first miracle, the turning of the water into wine at the marriage of Cana. Again, the kingly figure is important here. *Substance,* with seen and unseen properties—such as Christ's deity, the external and internal properties of the three kingly gifts, the nature of water being transformed into wine—is emphasized during the entire day of Epiphany. In its multilayered, multivalent significances, the entire day, from very early morning to night, ultimately exemplifies life in its multiplicity, as well as its inexorable ongoing motion. Further, as we will see, ways of moving and understanding can be seen within the *figurae* of the texts, whether one understands from the delineating *figurae* that the text is a plain statement of historical event, a "covering" for a hidden meaning (*integumentum*), a message to be taken seriously and followed (*tropus*, trope), or a statement concerning things to come. We will see how these modes alternate in constant alternation throughout this day, as it proceeds, note by note, letter of text by letter, to conclusion. This is an alternating principle of composition that is ubiquitous in the Middle Ages (*alternatim*). (See Editions: Music to Sing.)

Compare the edition with the English translation of the text in which a single topic, or a clear, delineatory figure gives identity to each chunk, or in the case of the manuscript illustration, portion. This is especially the case for the chunks that follow, not only for the Magnificat, but with those designated with names, such as "Magi," "First King," "Midwife," "Reporter." Both the edition and the pieces of music-text themselves clearly present chunks of sound material. This chunk structure is reinforced by the meaning of the text, in which each chunk presents a concise idea, a mental picture, or a self-contained thought. For music edition with Latin text, see Editions: Music to Sing. Compare the following:

English translations: At Vespers, at (over) the Psalm

Antiphon: With you at the beginning [in the day of your power, in the splendor of saints, from the womb before light was begotten]

Versiculus: The Kings of Tharsis and of the islands [offer gifts]

At the Magnificat

Antiphon: Your light comes, Jerusalem, and the glory of the Lord is over the earth and the people will walk in your light. Alleluia, world without end, amen.

Magnificat: canticle found in the Gospel of Luke 1, 46–55, sung at sunset:

> My soul has magnified the Lord,
> And my spirit has rejoiced in God my Saviour.
> For he has regarded the low estate of his handmaiden:
> For Behold, from henceforth all generations shall call me
>   blessed.
> For he that is mighty has done to me great things;
> and holy is his name.
> And his mercy is on them that fear him from generation to
>   generation.
> He has showed strength with his arm

He has scattered the proud in the imagination of their
  hearts.
He has put down the mighty from their seats,
And exalted them of low degree.
He has filled the hungry with good things;
And the rich he has sent empty away.
He has helped his servant Israel
In remembrance of his mercy
As he spoke to our fathers, to Abraham and to his seed
  forever.

This canticle, the Magnificat, sung at Vespers, toward the close of the
day, is an excellent example of the compositional method that we have
been considering, since it placed or ordered chunks, particularly of the
psalms, in this manner:

Psalm 35.9: And my soul shall be joyful in the Lord: it shall rejoice in
  his salvation
I Samuel I.11: remember me, and not forget thine handmaid
Malachi 3.12: And all nations shall call you blessed
Ps. 71.19: who has done great things
Ps. 99.3: Let them praise thy great and terrible name; for it is holy
Ps. 98.1: his right hand and his holy arm has gotten him the victory
Ps. 33.10–11: The Lord bringeth the counsel of the heathen to
  nought; he makes the devices of the people of none effect. The
  counsel of the Lord stands forever, the thoughts of his heart to
  all generations.

The singer of this song brought together building blocks from the
store of the Psalms and Old Testament books that was in her memory, so that the order, and the connection itself between the chunks
constituted the real work of the singer, in this case, Mary, the Mother
of Christ. Mary knew the psalms very well indeed. Medieval people
for the most part, especially those who could read and write, also
knew the Psalms. This way of composition, that is, selecting preexistent chunks and placing them thoughtfully and appropriately together, provided a method of working for the entire medieval period,
to be observed below in all of the chunks of *cantus* (or, in the common
English translation, "chant"). The Magnificat itself, since it was sung
on a daily basis at Vespers, or approximately sunset, constituted, in
turn, an available material to be worked over by composers for many
hundreds of years, as, for example, Johann Sebastian Bach's famous
Magnificat. (Notice here the chunks of text, as well as the interplay of

topics. Each chunk contains one implicit, *figura,* such as Christ, rock, waters, Jordan River, dove, gifts, king, etc. The *figura* also unifies the chunk, giving it focus, and making it memorable.) We continue with the service for Epiphany beginning with the offices and through what has become known as a "liturgical drama": verses before the celebra-· tion of the Mass.

At Matins

Invitatory verse: Christ appears to us: come, let us adore Him.

Psalm 94 (95): O Come let us sing unto the Lord;
let us make a joyful noise to the rock of our salvation;
Let us come before His presence with thanksgiving
and make a joyful noise unto Him with psalms.

[In the First Nocturne]

Antiphon: Bring to the Lord, the Son of God,
worship the Lord in His sanctuary

Antiphon: Mighty waters rejoice, alleluia (or the fount of
the waters rejoice)
in the city of God, alleluia.

Antiphon: Praise to our God,
Praise, praise, to our king,
Praise wisely! (that is, with understanding)

Responsory: Today in the Jordan [River] the Lord, baptized,
Opened up were the heavens
and then the Spirit as a dove remained over Him,
and the voice of the Father intoned,
"This is my beloved son, in whom I am well pleased."

Verse: The heavens were opened over Him,
and the voice of the Father was heard.

Responsory: Today the heavens were opened
and the sea was made sweet
the earth exalts and the countryside rejoices
as Christ was baptized by John in the Jordan.

Verse: What is it to you that the sea has fled away,
and that the Jordan has been turned around backwards?

Responsory: All they from Saba come bearing gold
   and incense
and praise to the Lord, proclaiming
Alleluia, alleluia, alleluia.

Verse: The kings of Tharsis and the islands bring
   presents,
the kings of Arabia and Saba bring gifts.

[In the Second Nocturne]

Antiphon: All the earth worships you and praises you,
It says a psalm in Your name, Lord. (note: the Latin
   dicat, meaning "it says," implies reading, saying,
   or singing)

Antiphon: The Kings of Tharsis and the islands
offer gifts to the Lord of Kings.

Antiphon: All people who You have made, come
and they will truly worship You, Lord

Versiculus: The Kings of Tharsis and of the islands
   [offer] gifts.

Responsory: The star which the magi saw
in the East went before them,
They came to the place where the young boy was.
Seeing also Him, rejoiced with great joy.

Verse: And entering the house,
they found the boy with Mary His mother
and proceeding, worshiped Him.

Responsory: The magi inquired of Herod:
what sign have you seen over the king that is born?
Burning brightly the great star,
whose splendor illuminates the earth,
and we ourselves recognize it and come,
to worship the Lord.

Verse: The magi came from the East, seeking the face
of the Lord and saying.

Responsory: Shine, Shine, Jerusalem
Your light has come
and the glory of the Lord has risen upon you.

Verse: And the people walked in your light
and Kings in the splendor of your place.

[In the Third Nocturne]

Antiphon: Come, let us adore Him, who Himself is our
Lord God.

Antiphon: Worship the Lord, Alleluia, all his angels,
alleluia.

Antiphon: Worship the Lord, alleluia, in His sanctuary,
alleluia.

Versiculus: All the people who You have made.

Responsory: The magi came from the East, Jerusalem,
Asking and saying
Where is He who is born,
Whose star we have seen?
And we have come to worship the Lord.

Verse: The magi came from the East.

Responsory: This holy day has shown upon us:
Come, people, and worship the Lord
For today a great light has appeared on the earth.

Verse: Come and worship Him, who Himself is our Lord God.

Responsory: As a kind of dove, the Holy Spirit was visible
The voice of God the Father was heard
"This is my beloved Son
In whom I am well-pleased, hear Him."

Verse: The heavens were opened over Him
And the voice of the Father was heard.

Responsory: Three are the precious gifts
Which the magi brought to the Lord, this day,
And they contain divine mysteries,
In gold is shown kingly power,
In incense, the office of a great priest,
and in myrrh, the Lord's burial place.

Verse: The magi venerated the author of our salvation,
      in a cradle
And from their mystical treasure,
Offered Him particular gifts.

Responsory: This is a glorious day,
In which the saviour of the world appears,
Whom the prophets foretold,
Angels worshipped,
Whose star the magi, seeing, rejoiced,
And offered their gifts.

Verse: And entering the house.

Responsory: Seeing the star, the magi
rejoiced with great joy
And entering the house
Found the young boy
With Mary, His mother,
And proceeding, worshipped Him
And opened their treasure,
Offering Him gifts, gold, incense, and myrrh.

Verse: The star which the magi saw in the East preceding them
And coming, remained over the place where the young
      boy was.

Responsory: A great king is born in Israel,
The kings of the earth came to worship the Lord,
And offered to Him,
Gifts of gold, incense, and myrrh.

Verse: The Kings of Tharsis.

Responsory: The kings of Tharsis and of the islands
      offered gifts
The kings of Arabia, and Saba
Brought presents to the Lord God.

Verse: And all of the kings will worship Him,
All the people will serve Him.

At Lauds

[Antiphon]: Lord before the creation of light, and before
    the world
Our saviour has appeared today to the world.

Antiphon: Three are the gifts that the magi offered to the Lord
Gold, incense, and myrrh,
To the Son of God, to the great king, alleluia.

Antiphon: Opened their treasure
The magi offered to the Lord
Gold, incense, and myrrh, Alleluia.

Antiphon: Mary and the river,
Bless the Lord,
Sing a hymn, the fount, to the Lord, Alleluia.

[Antiphon]: The magi, seeing the star,
Said to one another,
This is the sign of the great king,
We go and inquire of Him,
And offer to Him gifts, gold, incense, and myrrh.

Versiculus: All of Saba come.
At the Benedictus [Antiphon]:
Today the celestial bridegroom is united with the church,
When Christ washes sins in the Jordan,
As with gifts the magi hasten to the regal wedding,
And as water is made into wine, the company is
    gladdened, alleluia.

[At the Mass Celebration]

We believe the great king born with the star,
By whose eternal power the highest hosts are ruled
And by whose rule of love all throughout the ages are
    subdued.

Reporter: By a regal mandate, they announced, "hasten!"

Magi: Here, for Him made to reign, with mystical gifts
We come, the earth through, to worship.

Reporter: The king gives a command to us; all of the earth tremble
Step by step, directed to Him.

Magi: Now venerating [the one] holding the scepter, imperial king.

King: Tell me, my scribe, quickly, what is on the page?

Reporter: O opened law, cited by the king, with the line of the prophet, hastening, come.

King: O you scribe, being asked, say what it is concerning this child that you see written in the book?

Scribe: We see, Lord, in the line of the prophets, that it is clearly written.

Chorus: Bethlehem, not the least among the princes of Judah,
Out of you then will come a leader,
Who rules my people Israel,
Himself saving His people from their sins.

King: King, what do you seek?

Magi: Him who is born.

King: If He [is] to reign

King: Go, and concerning the boy

Magi: Here the star in the East

(*Aliter*: Another way) The First King:

The star shining brightly, glowing red

Second King: Showing where the king of kings was born

Third King: Whom prophecy signaled for the future,

All together: We therefore go and inquire concerning Him, offering to Him gifts, gold, incense, and myrrh.

Reporter: Then, the magi went and required star's direction
to the king who was born.

King: Tell before coming, what alone was known,
For what reason one came, what rumor did we need.

Reporter: Your rule

Magi: Now worshipping

King: King, whom do you seek, what sign do you say
    [signifies] the birth

Magi: We have said, a star showing, illuminated in the East.

King: If you believe Him to reign, tell us.

King: Here, my scribe.

King: Go and investigate diligently concerning the boy,
and finding Him, tell me.

Magi: Here the star in the East, shown the way,
a light went before us.

Midwife: Who are these, who the guiding star brought us,
bringing us inaudibly?

Magi responding together: We are, who you know to be the
    kings of Tharsis, Arabia, and Saba, offering gifts to Christ
    the King, born Lord,
Who, the star guiding, we come to worship.

Midwife: Here is the boy, whom you seek: now hasten,
Worship, who Himself is your redemption.

Magi together: Salve, king of the world.

First King: Accept now gold.

Second King: Take incense, Thou true God.

Third King: Myrrh, sign of the sepulcher.

Angel with a loud voice: Completed are all the things that
were foretold by the prophets.

Go, take another way, do not delay,
For you will be greatly punished by the king.

Magi: God be praised.
We praise Thee, O Lord.

Trope in the Epiphany of our Lord (*trope* uses an analogy, or metaphor, in order to make what has been said personal, with an implied personal application; a trope as a *figure* indicates the tropological sense or *mode.*)

Bridegroom of the church, illuminator of the people,
Sanctifier of baptism, redeemer of the world
Here He comes. Whom the kings of the gentiles
with mystical gifts, sought out Jerusalem, saying:
Where is the one who is born,
Lord of Lords?
We have seen his star in the East
And we have acknowledged Him to be born king of kings,
And His kingdom
Who alone should receive honor, praise, and jubilation,
And power. (Psalm). *Here He comes.*

(Portions in italic refer to chunks of the *Introit,* to which the analogy of the trope relates. Here we have two ways of understanding, made clear by the *figurae* at hand, that is, the way or tropological mode constituting an analogy with the literal mode of the *introit,* referring to the actual birth of Christ.)

Alleluia.

Pro sequentia: Sequence, or that which follows (this Sequence presents *figurae* that indicate clearly the allegorical, followed by the futuristic or eschatological modes. There are *figurae* from both Old and New Testaments, giving a transitional bridge between the Old Testament Hebrew word *Alleluia*, and the New Testament Gospel reading that is also known as "Sequentia"):

Praise, singing now a sweet song, a brotherly crowd
melody, rhythm, joined with the Lord
Who himself in his place of birth, Bethlehem

declares a new rule,
And today the mystic gifts of the magi are made congruent
    with him.
Rejoice, Bethlehem, city among the elected, as showing the
    amulet of the king
Here, Emmanuel, here Jesus, our life, the whole crowd
appropriates salvation.
What, Herod, seized by a rabid mind, taking, slaying those
    boys,
with whose demise the ages are bettered.
Not for your time arise dark purposes, but parallel future
    offspring in the mystery of the cross.
The children of Judah made hard, perpetually wounded,
By tears wiped away, lorded over, by so many crimes.
Rocks tremble, clattering: the veil is rent, divided,
Herod, you are sought; the Lord's funeral prepared.
For the ransom is sent, debt paid,
Who bears the sins of the world, planted in the flesh of the
    virgin;
Blessed body and mind brought up to the stars,
Where they retain joy remaining without end.

Alleluia.

Prosa (*Pro Sequentia*): We sing of the Lord's glorious
    Epiphany.
(again, the *sequentia* is filled with allegories, closing with
    the futuristic phrase):
Possessing power over the kingdom of this world,

He protects all, world without end.
Offertory: The kings of Tharsis and of the islands
offering gifts,
the kings of Arabia and Saba
bring gifts,
and worship him
all the kings of the earth,
all peoples serve him.
Verse: God of your judgment
and prince of your justice,
judge your people with justice
and your poor in judgment;
all peoples serve him.

Verse: The mountains bring forth peace for your people,
and the hills, justice.
Verse: To have risen, in that day, his justice,
and the abundance of peace,
Then the light is extolled,
and he will reign from sea to sea.

Sanctus: *Sanctus* (Holy): Merciful Sower of the word
whose palm is open for all,
Sanctus Merciful bough,
Light and coequal with light,
Sanctus Gracious purifier of all,
Paraclete, Atoner,
Lord, God of Sabaoth,
Filled with your glory are the heavens, and the Earth,
Hosanna, in the highest.

Agnus Dei: O Lamb of God [that takes away the sins of the
world].

The entire day through the medieval mass liturgy has been included for the following reasons. If one takes the trouble to carefully follow the entire program of events, which would have lasted from sunset January 5th throughout the day on January 6th, several aspects of composition and communication using sound substance become clear. First of all, the entire procession of events has been arranged in chunks. This becomes especially obvious as one uses one's breath to actually *sing* the antiphons, responsories, and all of the rest of the pieces, since each chunk just about expends a single breath, together with a single thought, an object to be imagined, or a single action. One learns about the construction of these pieces by doing—by actually experiencing the entire procession of events by singing them, one at a time, from beginning to end. This would be even more instructive if several people together would take on the project, especially since individual figures are sometimes given individual chunks or parts, and there is also a contrast between these single figures and the chorus (or *turba, agmina*). The entire edition, with translations, have been included here for just that purpose, so that one can actually *experience* the Day of Epiphany to as close an extent as possible, as it was presented at a 12th-century French cathedral that, at least since the final generation of the 9th century, also had a distinguished and long-standing cathedral school.

In looking closely at this day of events, we see that each chunk encloses, or contains, a single figure, such as king, the imagined kings of

Tharsis, the islands, Arabia, and Saba. In addition to a kingly figure, exotic places "to the East" are brought into the inner place of the imagination. Light, the city of Jerusalem, and so on, one by one, throughout the entire procession of varied and diverse figures, constitute an alphabet of *figurae* from beginning to end. On the basis of each figure, one can discern the motion of that particular chunk, whether the motion (or mode) presents an event to be taken at face value; a hidden meaning or allegory,; a message to be taken personally and applied to one's own life, that is, a tropology (*tropus*); or the end of time, the end of the world, or the end of one's own life, that is, a futuristic mode. A perceptible pattern of alternation has also been consciously set up. The deaths of the innocent boys killed by King Herod would have been regarded as expressing the historical or literal way, or mode, of understanding. Next, the futuristic mode, referring to Christ's death in the future, or the presence of an entire crowd before God at the end of time is introduced. The futuristic mode is also characteristic, for example, of the final lines of the Sequence. The allegorical mode is perhaps the most difficult to deal with since the figures present, on the surface, a "covering" for what is actually signified—a meaning that must be thought about, and reflected upon, before it becomes clear. And finally, there are also many analogies, or tropes, interfaced with the Introit, *Here he comes*. If we consider the celebration of the mass liturgy beginning with the "Trope in the Epiphany of our Lord," the literal mode is invoked in the Introit, *Here he comes*. Then there are also analogies or tropes, such as: "Bridegroom of the church," "Illuminator of the people," "Sanctifier of baptism," and "Redeemer of the world." The sequence, as well, which follows, expresses first the historical mode, in terms of place and situation, namely, Bethlehem, culminating with the futuristic mode: "Blessed body and mind brought up to the stars/ Where they retain joy remaining without end."

An imagined and expected future is brought to mind in terms of the Christian's presence before God within a large company. And so it goes, throughout the entire day, one way of moving or mode followed by the other. The reader, and especially the singer, is refreshed by the constant alternation of ways of proceeding and understanding, and also by the constant alternation of figures. In a sense, the order of events is very much like a jazz performance in which a different instrument, say, the saxophone, alternates with another, the trumpet or percussion, and each instrument (or *figura*) has its say, one after the other, in alternation.

Nearly all of the chunks, furthermore, could be found elsewhere, as chunks taken out of their context, especially within the Book of Psalms, the prophetic books of the Old Testament, such as Isaiah, or the New Testament, in this case, especially, the Gospels. Preexistent material has been chopped up into chunks and repositioned, replaced, and re-combined. One also has the impression that each one of the pieces con-stitutes a variation on the others, that the same topics—such as the kings from the East (Matthew 2.1–12), the baptism of Christ in the Jor-dan River (Matthew 3.13–17; Mark 1.9–11, Luke 2.21–27), the star shin-ing brightly (cf. Numbers 24.17), the figure of Herod the king, the gifts, and the marriage at Cana (John 2.1–11)—appear, then appear again in slightly different configuration, and then reappear yet again. These topics also alternate passages from the Gospels from which they were taken. Finally, order is individual and could even be personal. The chunks are autonomous; one might even consider them to be modular, so that they could be reseparated and reconnected in slightly differ-ent order. And the order changes, as well, if one chunk is transferred to another position within the entire procession of events. This dif-ference, quite specifically, in the order itself is often the crucial differ-ence between one responsory and another. Further, there are simple, straightforward, features—such as "star," "gifts," "the king"—that can be understood by a child and that remain as clear, perceptible figures in the memory of children. From these features, however, one can con-tinue, if one is able, from a consideration of recognizable, particular things, placed in a familiar order, moving from one object to the next, to an understanding that is far more difficult to acquire of such issues as the "substance" of God, as revealed in Christ; intention and motiva-tion as an abstraction, but in this case related to the inner and outward movement of the kings of the East; the theological implications of bap-tism arising from historical precedent within Jewish practice; and the nature of the "substance" of water turned into wine—even transfor-mation itself of basic *materia/substantia* of water/wine—that is, what actually happened, how, and why this took place. These, of course, are only a few of the questions to be considered within the disciplines of theology and philosophy that are divided today but which coincided with one another and were, in fact, inseparable in the Middle Ages, and as principles, they found exemplification within the discipline of music.

We have seen all of this before. All of these features of figure, mode, chunks, order, and preexistent material were examined and commented upon in the discussion on "Fiordinando." But there is another observa-tion that must be made. The entire processionality of all of the pieces in an order provides a clear illustration of those principles of particular-ity, connection, and motion that a medieval person studied in school. Note by note, relationship by relationship, moving right along from late afternoon of one winter's day to the night of the next (Epiphany), abstract concepts of particular sound body—a tone—united with the next enclosed sound body, showing relationship and appropriateness, as well as the nature of movement itself, became experiential. A system of learning could be fully understood because it was applied in very conscious ways to life, even as this "system" was *sung*.

We have confronted another mental culture, not to remark upon how obsolete it might seem, but to learn from it. As with all cultures to which we are not accustomed, we find some aspects that seem strange, even irrelevant, and others that seem so self-evident as to be boring. Seen and experienced from the outside, the particular, even peculiar, combination of the exotic, the boring, the tedious, and the newly discovered is what gives any culture its uniqueness. We can also be expanded by such a confrontation and should not give up if it requires patience and effort on our part. But one other considerable reason why it is not easy to understand another culture—one that we do not intuitively know from years of experience within that culture—is one of separation and joining. Medieval mental culture for the period we have been discussing, for example, so far as we are able to tell, makes no separation between "sacred" and "secular" but looks, rather, at life as unified. What one might regard today as "secular" education, as completely disassociated from going to church, practicing a religious faith, or observing a family background that includes traditional religious customs, is not at all the case for the mental environment we have been discussing. Rather, the principles one learned in school, for example, of particular letters of the alphabet, or the quality of a single number, were all strengthened by singing particular notes and the recognition of the particular and unique sounds of tones as one sang during a church service. An illustration of the basic principles of particularity (individual tones), relationship (tones associated in melodies), and motion (movement was made clear as one sang one tone after another), was offered, and reinforced, by the service for Epiphany or the Celebration of the Three Kings. Another separation that we, perhaps, take for granted, namely, the division made between "folk" and "art" music, is also not to be found in medieval mental culture. Still another separation that is common today, but not to this mental frame of mind, is the distinct separation between knowledge and life. If one couldn't apply what one had learned in some way to life, it wasn't worth much, and if one couldn't apply what one had learned to life, one hadn't really learned much.

We are traveling, in a sense, into a distant land, but with the point of view that, perhaps, there is something to be learned there, that insights from the people of the Middle Ages can teach us something, and that, at any rate, we are able to understand ourselves and our own mental, spiritual, and intellectual environments the better for having been elsewhere.

In summary of a background of medieval intellectual culture, we began with a "folktale" selected in this context because it contains chunks of material, clearly perceptible within the continuity of a narrative or story. The motion of the story, or *figurae*, also itself in turn served as a repository for future renditions, and the entire collection of "folktales" serves as well as a repository of substance—of stuff—from which one could help oneself in order to put together one's own work. Nerucci's notes on the "dissemination" of this tale, contained within his volume of "folktales" are of interest here. The kingly figure was important for all of these tales recomposed and collected into his volume, and this is also true of the one considered here.

Secondly, a medieval conceptualization of material was emphasized as the "forest" (the Latin word *silva*), full of trees, a resource to be appropriated and used, separated out into manageable logs, branches, and pieces. Concepts become objects for the medieval mind; there is no difference, in other words, between working with visible material and working with material that is conceptual and emotional. This unification constitutes one of the most important aspects of medieval mentality. Chunks of building substance were placed side by side within a composition process, and the considerable mastery needed to bring these chunks together constituted the work of the artist or the scientist as one who knows how to deal with available material, both visible and conceptual.

The question comes then to mind: What substance was in this *silva*, or forest full of useful material? What had they accumulated, to be used as they wished, and according to the mastery each one possessed? Some of the most important concepts and ideas have been selected here from a truly vast "forest" of material available to the composer, working with sound—particularized into words and tones. The fact that sound is the substance of both words and music, noted by both Quintilian and Augustine as well as many others, was not lost on medieval composers. The "stuff" of sound, the nature of stuff, the stuff of nature are all preoccupations of writers within this period. We have attempted to find out what they thought about making, actualizing, and experiencing compositions, and even the act itself of thinking about them, beforehand, as well as in retrospect. The background to this concept includes Cicero and his concept of the *occasion* as a delimited chunk of time; Virgil and his pieces of thought, contained within motion, particularly within his great epic, the *Aeneid*, that so much influenced medieval mental civilization, since it was known, no doubt, in a large part by memory; Quintilian and his books on communication; Augustine and his concept of *pulse* as an enclosed piece of sound; the Book of Psalms and the chunk-like portions throughout the

Book of Psalms; as well as the use of these chunk-like portions used for *cantus*.

All of these authors were so well-known during the centuries of the Middle Ages that most people who had what would have been a high school diploma today could quote large passages of the Psalms by memory. In fact, those who could read at all knew the Psalms by memory, so that the language, construction, thought-framework, concepts, and genres of the Psalms were ubiquitous during the Middle Ages and beyond, at least into the 18th century. By reading these authors and acknowledging their influence upon the Middle Ages, we become acquainted with concepts that underlie medieval communication and artistic production (i.e., material, preexistent material, material chunk, figure, varied and diverse figures, and figures within motion).

In effect, "Fiordinando" could also have been entitled "The Forest." This story has be used with the purpose in mind of introducing all of the necessary concepts, as well as ways in which these concepts are expressed—and understood—in both English and Latin terms. In dealing with both composition and communication, we are dealing with arts that are normally separated today but were in the Middle Ages united by common materials to be used, constructional structures, and ways of operation. How this common structure and vocabulary was translated into, and greatly influenced by, rhetorical, political, or forensic speeches; music; as well as the visual arts, is impossible to understand without a consideration of the background understood during that time. This is the reason why the artistic culture of the Middle Ages in its widest sense has not necessarily been understood in the 20th century but, rather, has been commonly viewed as derivative.[12] Medieval constructional principles and a mentality that not only include recombination but finds recombination self-evident and essential, can be seen in the included Mass for Epiphany including tropes and a "liturgical drama," as it became known at Nevers Cathedral in early 12th century. This service illustrates the concept of "chunks" and exemplifies how the concepts discussed here could be (and were) actualized within performance. All of the aspects that have been initially presented within a narrative will be discussed in more detail in the chapters that follow.

Fig. 4.1 Manuscript, "Vergilius Romanus," folio 44v (cf. Sabine MacCormack, *The Shadows of Poetry: Vergil in the Mind of Augustine* [Berkeley/Los Angeles, 1998], p. 8.)

Fig. 4.2 Virgil seated on his throne, folio 3v, ca. fifth century (kingly figure as a heritage throughout this period under discussion). Note that no difference has been made between "objects" and "texts"—both were composed of placed-together pieces of material. (cf. Sabine MacCormack, *The Shadows of Poetry: Vergil in the Mind of Augustine* [Berkeley/Los Angeles, 1998].)

Fig. 4.3 Building blocks from a Roman past, used, chunk-by-chunk, as "available pre-existent material" for centuries, even today. (Blocks within the city's Roman Museum in which Roman blocks have been reintegrated into a contemporary edifice, Cologne, Germany.) (Photograph by the author.)

Fig. 4.4 David the King, thought to be the composer of the Psalms, often is depicted at the beginning of the Book of Psalms (the *"Beatus"* initial). This example is taken from Koblenz, Staatsarchiv Manuscript 710, Nr. 110, f. 153v, an incomplete Bible. The initial begins the Book of Psalms (*Liber psalmorum*). The inscription is telling: *David psalmografus in tactus spiritus almi/Christo psalterio psallebat et in monocordo/Et fera dulcisonis de mulcens pectora verbis.* (David the psalmist the spirit-touched soul, by the Psalter of Christ in [use of] the monochord, by sweet sound with word, stroking the heart). The Book of Psalms brought together the Old and the New Testaments, David and Christ. (Used by permission, Koblenz, Staatsarchiv.)

Fig.4.5 *B* of the *Beatus vir* (Blessed is the Man) opening the St. Omer Psalter, now in London, British Library, Manuscript Yates Thompson 14, f. 74 (see also F. O. Büttner, "Der illuminierte Psalter im Westen," in *The Illuminated Psalter: Studies in the Content, Purpose and Placement of its Images*, ed. F. O. Büttner [Turnhout, 2004], p. 50. [c] The British Library Board.)

Fig. 4.6 Gradual: *Beatus vir, qui timet Dominum.* (From *Liber usualis,* Book for use).

Fig. 4.7 "Alleluia" with its verse from the Psalms, *Beatus vir, qui timet Dominum.* (From *Liber usualis,* Book for use).

Fig. 4.8 Tract: *Beatus vir qui timet Dominum,* with verses *Potens in terra erit* and *Gloria et divitiae in domo ejus.* (From *Liber usualis,* Book for use).

Fig. 4.9 An example of the first of a now famous series of illustrations from manuscript Paris, Bibliothèque nationale, fonds Latin, Ms 1118, folios 104, 105v, 106v, 107v, 109, 110, 111, all of which together illustrate the concept of *figura in modis* as well as the topic of "varied and diverse figures" (*figurae variarae*). This series is accompanied by music notational *figurae*, showing how distinctive *figurae* indicate ways, manners of moving, or *modi* within material. The "Primus," no doubt, David the King and musician of the Psalms, initiates the series. The King is seated next to *cantus* that expresses the first mode, the *primus*. (Used by permission, Paris, Bibliothèque nationale.)

Fig. 4.10 The *Roman de Fauvel*, Bibliothèque nationale, fonds fr. (French Collection), 146, indicating *figura, figurae in modis* (modes of text, music, drawing), and varied and diverse *figurae*, or *charactere variarae* (*charivari*). (Used by permission, Paris, Bibliothèque nationale.)

Fig. 4.11 The *Roman de Fauvel*, Bibliothèque nationale, fonds fr. (French Collection), 146, indicating *figura; figurae in modis* (modes of text, music, drawing); and varied and diverse *figurae*, or *charactere variarae* (*charivari*). (Used by permission, Paris, Bibliothèque nationale.)

Fig. 4.12 Florence, Biblioteca Laurentiana Ms 29.1, facsimile ed. Luther A. Dittmer, 2 vols. (Used by permission, Publications of Medieval Musical Manuscripts, 10 [Brooklyn, New York, n/d]. Used by permission.)

NOTES

1. It is interesting to reflect that while numbers (within the particularity discipline of arithmetic) do not need sound, alphabetical letters ultimately do require, as well as use, sound. (One can even say that as one reads silently, one imagines sound—that is, pronunciation.) The presence or absence of sound as a crucial difference is maintained throughout all of the three communicational disciplines in contrast to the "material and measurement" disciplines. This becomes an noteworthy observation as one examines the function of music within that context, as a "sound discipline" within the context of the "material and measurement" disciplines that essentially do not require sound.

2. See Quintilian, *Institutio oratoria*, I.viii.16: *schemata utraque, id est figuras . . .* (schemata or figures known as figures of speech and figures of thought). The most recent edition of Cassiodorus's Psalm Commentaries, which abound in varied and diverse *figurae*, points these out by the addition of SCHE (*schemata*) in the margins. See Magni Aurelii Cassiodori, *Expositio psalmorum*, 2 vols., ed. Martin Adriaen, *Corpus christianorum series latina* (CCSL) (Turnhout, 1958).

3. The Greek *pathos* can be, and was, translated into Latin as *passio/passiones, modus/modi,* or *affectus/affectiones* as ways/manners of movement indicated by pertinent, indicatory *figurae*.

4. The contrast of the single *figura*, or *simplex*, and varied and diverse *figurae*, or *charactere variare*, is a contrast maintained throughout the Middle Ages, for many purposes and in many contexts, as we will see.

5. See articles *de Ordine, de Musica*, in *Augustine through the Ages. An Encyclopedia*, ed. Allan D. Fitzgerald, O.S.A. (Grand Rapids, Michigan, 1999).

6. Augustine, at the time of his conversion to Christianity, ca. 387, wrote four seminal treatises that, rather than youthful writings from which he quickly moved on, constituted a basis for the writing projects that would continue throughout his long life. These treatises include: "The Qualities and Quantities of the Soul" (or treatises on the subject of "soulish substance"), "The Order that Exists within the Disciplines," and a treatise on music (see chapter VI, "They All Read the Same Books").

7. Aristotle goes into this aspect of "soulish substance" especially in *De anima*, "Concerning the Substance of the Soul," which was translated, made available to university discussion, and had increasing importance as witnessed by commentaries on it from the last generation of the 13th century on.

8. For a useful summary of specific translations of Aristotle's works, as well as when each became available and studied, see Bernard G. Dod, "Aristoteles latinus," in *Cambridge History of Later Medieval Philosophy* (Cambridge, UK, 1982), pp. 45–79, especially the table of medieval Latin translations and their influence (pp. 74–79).

9. These treatises are mentioned in the order of their available translation, beginning with the late 12th century and continuing through the 13th century; all Aristotle's treatises provided examples of his basic principles, contained in the *Metaphysics*, were influential to an enormous extent, and continued to attract commentaries, as is readily apparent by consulting library catalogues particularly of major European libraries and their present holdings. Even

works Aristotle did not write received attention from the 13th century on, such as the "Secret of Secrets" (*Secretum*), falsely attributed to Aristotle as "The Philosopher's advice on life to his pupil Alexander the Great."

10. See van Deusen, "Roger Bacon on Music" in: *Roger Bacon and the Sciences,* ed. Jeremiah Hackett (Leiden, 1997), pp. 223–241, p. 226: "Both Augustine and Bacon thought that music was important since music was both useful and necessary, not only in understanding the essential principles of other allied disciplines, but in understanding what they considered to be ultimate realities, namely, God and the human soul."

11. Leonardo da Vinci in particular (although he was not the first), argues that since drawing made both substance and life plain, it should take the place of music as the exemplary discipline.

12. This is an attitude expressed even by those who study the Middle Ages, who view it as unoriginal and repetitive, hence, uninteresting. (Mark Whittow, for example, in his book, *The Making of Byzantium 600–1025,* published Cambridge, UK, in 1996, regards Byzantine chronicles and histories as presenting "coverage that is patchy, they are often written long after the event, and they are frequently distorted by a propagandist bias" (p. 7,9). He notes elsewhere: "Apart from the uneven coverage, the main problem with all these texts is their obvious unreliability.") The entire introductory chapter is important for this discussion.

5

Silva: Inner and Outer Substance, Music, and Material Culture

Let us start anew, bringing out in detail each one of the aspects introduced within the overview. We begin with a notion of stuff and Plato's *Timaeus*. Not only was Plato's text of great importance in the Middle Ages but also the priorities explained by the commentary from Chalcidius, who translated the *Timaeus* from Greek into Latin. The influence of the *Timaeus* was great from the early to the later centuries of the Middle Ages. We know this for certain from the manuscripts in libraries still available today.[1] It appears that nearly every medieval library of any note had at least one, if not several, copies of the Latin translation of the *Timaeus*, often with the commentary by Chalcidius as well. This commentary makes Chalcidius's priorities plain as he interacts with Plato's writing. Further, Chalcidius's attention to and discussion of the topics he has selected as important, also provided a collection of terms and concepts that remained central throughout the Middle Ages, influencing how music was regarded, its disciplinary function, and its position relative the other disciplines that made up a well-organized educational system.

With the *Timaeus* in hand, one needed to look no further to fix the boundaries, settle the issues, and decide on terms to be used to open up for inspection what we might call a medieval mentality, as well as the place of music within this mentality and to what its principal terms refer. We are dealing here with a mental culture to explain the world in which one lived, both in terms of invisible as well as visible reality, and to make this world comprehensible, even to young students. One should also add in this context that there is, perhaps, no factor that divides cultures—both geographical as well as temporal—as decisively as the topic treated by the *Timaeus*, namely, material (*materia/substantia/natura*): of what it consists, how to describe it, and how to work effectively with it.

What, indeed, is "stuff?" Where does it come from, how can one approach and describe it, what can one do with it? Does "stuff" concern only what one can see, touch, handle, weigh, and throw away? What one regards as material in nature has a good deal to do with what one values, prizes, and respects, whether visible or invisible. We will go after what can be regarded as the predominant value contained within the *Timaeus* as presented in the Latin translation of that work and show how this value was expressed and exemplified in music and how it provided a basis for the study of music in its fullest sense.

Plato begins with notions of *prior* and *posterior,* as successive numbers within time, and with the notion of memory as occurring within time, as past and present (*in tempore*),[2] directly contrasting with what is taken up later on as "what is that which is Existent always, and has no Becoming."[3] But furthermore the readers of the *Timaeus* are presented with what, on reflection, might be considered to be self-evident, namely, that seeing is believing. According to the *Timaeus,* the sense of sight is the first sense, both for making one's way in the world, as well as feeling at ease about it. The sense of sight reinforces what is seen; repetition through seen objects, recurring in customary ways, through familiarity, console us with a sense that all is well with the world. Seen repetition reassures us with the pleasure of recognition and a sense of comfort.

All this is true, and its obviousness would indicate that the sense of hearing, and in conjunction with that sense, music, would take a second place, serve a secondary function during the period of time during the Middle Ages when the *Timaeus,* in its partial Latin translation with copious commentary by Chalcidius, continued to be read and thought about in terms of further commentaries. It is worth noting again that there is every indication that the *Timaeus,* in its Latin translation, was enormously influential in the Middle Ages: it presented an arsenal of conceptual tools with which to access and deal with basic principles regarding matter, generation, and life; a vocabulary of Latin terms of great usefulness in approaching these concepts; and a platform, so to speak, for initiating further discussion concerning these issues and words.[4]

What we have mentioned, namely, that hearing is a second-class sense, and sound, as well as music, is of lesser consequence than sight, was, however, oddly enough, not accepted as a premise, in subsequent interaction with, and extension of, the Latin *Timaeus* and its commentary within medieval mental culture. An indication of the dignity, importance, and ultimate functionality of hearing and music as the first sense within medieval disciplines, is that, still, many centuries later, Leonardo da Vinci in his writings on art criticism complained with some bitterness that since the visual arts served the same function as music, that is, making profound, basic, philosophical concepts available to the senses; drawing, in particular, should hold the same place and acquire the same dignity as an indispensable discipline as music. Drawn *figurae*, since they carefully depicted life itself, should also be considered a material and measurement discipline, just as music—or even in place of music.[5] I mention this since the entire discussion by da Vinci, to which he obviously gives a good deal of effort, shows just how important the material of sound, its shaped organization into music, as well as the sense of hearing—all incorporated into a carefully structured discipline—were for many hundreds of years. Music in the Middle Ages, and actually much later than what is customarily considered to be the medieval period, was a *material* discipline, making *plain* what material was, its properties, how it could be used, and precisely what measurements could be applied to it.

Paradoxically, music—and the intellectual culture of the Middle Ages—had the Latin *Timaeus* and its fourth-century translator Chalcidius to thank for this perception of its nature. The *Timaeus* delineated not only how one should think about material but how to recognize it. And this is an example, as well, of the power of translation itself, the influence of the choice of concept on the part of the translator, and, further, a clear example of the translational process in that the translator also infuses terms with what he himself knows, believes he knows, and believes to be true. The translation itself, in addition to providing, case by case, metaphors for terms (*translatio*), constitutes a *composite*— a composition—on the part of the translator. This chapter will take up the Latin *Timaeus*, its transmission particularly through the commentary of Chalcidius, and how this translation, by means of just one particular intellectual sleight of hand, profoundly shaped the discipline of music throughout the Middle Ages, reaching to the present. The view of sound as substantial has influenced ways in which music is taught, even unconsciously, but with full acceptance, today, since basic musicianship is commonly taught at conservatories to undergraduates as "the materials of music."

As has been observed, nearly every medieval library of note had at least one copy, if not multiple copies, of the Latin translation of the *Timaeus* by Chalcidius, frequently also with the commentary by this translator. In a sense, one need look no further to make progress in determining a "medieval mentality." We have it right here in the translation of and commentary on the *Timaeus*.[6] Medieval readers all read the same books, and one of these, certainly, was the *Timaeus latinus*. So, it should be taken seriously. Even Marsilius Ficino, who translated the works of Plato in the late 15th century, departed very little from the text Chalcidius had translated. It seems that we have a great deal of help in accessing what medieval people—shall we say from around the beginning of the 9th century to at least the end of the 14th—thought about and how they captured these thoughts in language, so far-reaching and comprehensive is the influence of the Latin *Timaeus*. What did its readership make of this work, and what priorities did they select? How did the Latin *Timaeus* differ from Plato's Greek thoughts or concepts, shaped by the Greek language and its history? Furthermore, did the Latin *Timaeus* depart, as well, from a pre-Socratic, as well as a Platonic tradition, and what difference did this make specifically for what can be called a Latinized medieval culture thinking, writing, even speaking the Latin language a good deal of the time? These are comprehensive questions that are not easily answered, but by selecting one important issue to be found in the *Timaeus*, we may be able to make some progress. We can provide a platform for further discussion of music within medieval thought. We will draw attention, first of all, to the importance of the Latin translation with commentary for a medieval culture of the mind; secondly, we will point out one specific priority within this translational project; and thirdly, we will observe the application of this priority within the emerging material discipline of music.

Unfortunately, the issues that might contain the answers to these questions are not so interesting these days. What both Plato and Chalcidius, as well as many commentators, all have to say about these issues, are very nearly incomprehensible, perhaps, to educated people today—indicating just how far removed an early 21st-century mental culture might be from those who, for centuries, explained the world in which they were living by means of the vocabulary and conceptualization offered them by the Latin *Timaeus*. We have observed that perhaps no other topic separates physical and temporal cultures more than a prevailing assessment of *material* and its features—of what *stuff* consists; how one regards material; what types of material are indeed valued, for what reasons and for itself; of what its properties consist; as well as these properties' inherent functionality, that is, what these properties are "good for." This is also the topic of "goods," or a consideration of material reality, also the priority of Aristotle, especially in the *Physics*. An attitude towards substantial/material reality also fashioned and validated the discipline of music, as well as an attitude toward what music comprised and its specific area of usefulness in the Middle Ages. Music's own challenge and opportunity was—and is— to effectively exemplify basic concepts.

The primary consideration, then, of the *Timaeus* is, broadly delineated, material, and it is just this subject upon which both its Greek as well as its Latin readers were divided, namely, on the topic of material reality, a priority of both Plato and Aristotle (and even more so in the subsequence transformation of Plato's text by Chalcidius, who, as we will see, apparently regarded sound, hence music, as a valuable exemplification of invisible, yet material, reality).

Hyle, the Greek term for what exists, being, or, also, "stuff," is Plato's point of beginning and key to the argumentation of the *Timaeus*. It does not take either Plato or Chalcidius long to get into this concept. At the same time, what Chalcidius makes of this concept, as well as the importance he grants it, and the direction in which he points the term indicate Chalcidius's priority and his specific contribution to Plato's writing. *Hyle*, for Chalcidius, is *chaos*,[7] but he does not refer particularly or exclusively to stuff that can be seen, heard, noticed, and molded in some way. *Hyle* is, most importantly, invisible yet substantial material. The debate on this subject of *hyle* is, and was, even at the time of the translation of the *Timaeus* into Latin, vast. Chalcidius seems to have avoided the no-doubt irreconcilable larger issues and, quite simply, tells us that he took the term and translated it, necessarily, as he states, into a perfectly useable and ordinary Latin expression, *silva*—"necessitatem porro nunc appellat hylen, quam nos Latine silvam possumus nominare"[8]—and again, *chaos*—"quam Graeci hylen, nos silvam vocamus."[9] (*Silva*, necessarily now called *hyle*, which we Latins are able to name *silva*, and *chaos*, the Greek *hyle*, we call *silva*).

This seems to be a rather harmless exchange, not worth going into in too much detail, supported, as Chalcidius states, by Pythagoras. Yet the implications of what, in some sense, is a translational sleight of hand are enormous. These implications of Chalcidius's *silva* are contradictory to one of the basic theses of the Greek *Timaeus*, that is, that what is seen has priority over what is invisible, yet present, as *sound*. In some ways a typical Greek expression implying almost everything, and at the same time delivering almost nothing to hold securely in one's grasp—namely, all of the stuff around and everywhere, existing forever, both seen and unseen—is channeled very consciously by Chalcidius into a "forest full of trees," and therefore the expression is demythologized, so to speak. A demystification process has taken place by this *translatio*, or metaphor. The Greek *hyle* is made into an ordinary, concrete, and more comprehensible Latin *silva*. This translation of an already transliterated *hyle* was, after all, unnecessary, since the Latin language was already, by the time of Chalcidius's writing, full of Greek terms. (It is always less difficult to insert a convenient and meaningful term from another language than to search for an adequate expression in the language one is using, as, for example, the easy, everyday use in English of such foreign words as gemütlichkeit, zeitgeist, angst, raison

d'être, or laissez-faire.) The treasure of Greek conceptual terminology
had long since been plundered by Latin writers searching for words.
Chalcidius could have followed suit. He did not, and he proceeded to
devote the major portion of his commentary that followed to explain
himself, thus indicating that the transformation he had effected was
not as matter-of-fact as it might on the surface seem.

Silva—a forest full of trees; a rich source of material that could be accessed and appropriated. Depending upon innate properties, at least
part of the trees in the forest would die, becoming yet another kind of
material. Chalcidius's use of *silva* transformed the concept into one
that could be directed to very specific uses. Not only was this repository of the "forest" useful, but it was vast and without limitations—a
dark, even opaque, disorderly thicket; a maze; an intense, compact texture, full of potentially useful material.

We have already considered this forest. *Silva* invited those who
knew of its existence and who could work with its material properties to enter and help themselves. The possibilities for differentiation
into characteristic *figurae* or *differentiae*—figures and differences—were
endless. The concept of *silva*, therefore, contained within itself *differentiation*, made clear by *indicators*. All of these are patently and ultimately
real: their reality extended also to the reality within the imagination.[10]

In other words, *silva* itself is infinite and indeterminate—limitless
stuff—but this stuff could be differentiated by *figurae* into *modi*, or clas-
sifiable *motions* of difference (*differentiae*). These "ways of moving"
using essentially the same *materia* but with differences are made clear
by *figurae*. One question, of course, that immediately comes to mind
is how, in fact, did Chalcidius come to, and settle upon, this particular word in the Latin language. There was precedent for this term, as
Chalcidius also writes. However, the fact that Chalcidius selected *silva*,
with its obvious material connotations, illustrates what occurred in the
translational process here, namely, that Chalcidius appropriated from
many sources (in particular, the discussion of material and its properties from Aristotle's *Physics*)[11] all of the aspects of material property
he could think of, and loaded them into *silva*. In a sense, then, *silva* as
a word itself is an example of what the word signifies, namely, an entire thicket of aspects, concepts, permutations, and threads, a preexistent conceptual *stuff* from which one could take out and select what
was useful to one's own purposes. Chalcidius's *silva* itself is a collection and *composition*, a *composite* from many different sources that were
available to him at that time.

The passages on the subject of *silva* make up a substantial portion and major contribution of Chalcidius's entire work. Although
Chalcidius's quotations from the *Timaeus*, and commentary on these

quotations are channeled to some extent by the directionality and progression of topics within Plato's Greek text, as Plato brings them up,
one after the other, the section on *silva* is the most prominent indication of Chalcidius's own priorities, giving a foundation to medieval
mentality. If this were not the case, would not have taken such pains
to explain himself.[12]

Here is what happens. One moves from one topic to another in this
sequence. Chalcidius, taking on the Greek text, has been discussing
anima, and the interrelationship of *anima* with *corpus*, that is, "soul/
mind" and "body," arriving then at a section entitled "in praise of seeing," *Laus videndi*. The reader moves from what is unseen to the seen,
and the capacity for sight, a subject that, in spite of his words of praise,
Chalcidius immediately abandons with the no-nonsense statement,
"and now we will examine another sense." There are two senses, he
states, sight and hearing, by which we can comprehend things, and
which also instruct us when those things are no longer directly present.[13] A translation of Plato's text then follows: "How much, by means
of the utility of the voice, is grasped through music; and all of what the
human race consists can be attributed to *harmonia*" (this, by the way,
is an obvious example of an extremely important Greek term simply
downloaded, so to speak, into the Latin language and used, although,
as Chalcidius also states, *harmonia* has indeed a Latin translation, *modulatio*).[14] The Latin text is: "Quantumque per vocem utilitatis capitur ex
musica, totum hoc constat hominum generi propter harmoniam tribu-
tum," to which Chalcidius responds in his comment, that a harmonic
ratio has been built between mind on top (*in superioribus*) and nature,
which can be said to consist of the motion of the rhythmic modes or
"manners of moving." This is, again, a translational dilemma, since
the language used here is at the same time too familiar to music historians today who are acquainted with what has become by now a
conventional music theoretical terminology. On the other hand, *harmonia* in this context is quite incomprehensible. We may be lulled by
what we perceive as convention and familiar expressions into believing that we understand the point that Chalcidius is making here. This
point, to become so influential throughout the Middle Ages, is that
the various delineations of predictable movement found in recognizable rhythmic patterns negotiate a bridge between what is sensed and
what is known, between *natura*, or that of which the world consists,
and its sensory perceptions. The bridge made of musical sound is that
link between the perceived realities of the physical world and unseen
yet substantial reality. Chalcidius goes on to say that this, in fact, is
the measure of music's great importance, not so much on account
of its magical properties that cause people in general (the *vulgus*) to

absolutely lust after it (*non in ea qua vulgus delectatur quaeque ad volup-tatem facta excitat*), but that music partakes somehow of the divine, in that through music, reason and intellectual undertaking are no longer separated from sensorially perceived, strongly insistent reality. A con-sensual *symphonia* ensues as mind-spirit (*anima*) is brought back to its proper path, literally, *a via recta*.[15] Chalcidius states:

> This, indeed, is an optimal *symphonia* within our system of law and principle, from whence both reward and works proceed. For reason is leader; there is an inner vigor, similar to rage, in its strength and inti-macy, but much more productive than rage, providing a helping hand to the will. Without this modulating, harmonizing, force [—that is, the reconciliation of opposites—] from whence music follows, and by which music consists—there is no *symphonia*; and without *symphonia*, there is no music. For without a doubt, music clothes the mind-spirit with ratio-nality, recalling the spirit to itself and its internal properties also from that time when God fashioned the world.

Chalcidius closes with "All music is posited in voice, in hearing, and in sound. By sense, then, concept becomes known within intelligi-ble things. Music's usefulness therefore is that by this aural sense, *all* of philosophy becomes comprehensible—all philosophy can be notated as intelligible reality." (Latin: "Tota porro musica in voce et auditu et sonis posita est. Utilis ergo etiam iste sensus est philosophiae totius as-secutioni ad notationem intellegibilis rei.")[16]

Silva, as the editor of the *Timaeus latinus* notes in his chapter head-ing, follows, for at least the next 73 pages in our modern edition, as Chalcidius gives the reader a real tour-de-force of what *silva* contains, what could be done with this stuff. At the same time he is providing a vocabulary for the discipline of music for the next one and one-half millennia, as we see in the passage given in note 15. We are led from the unseen, vivifying force of the world, essentially unlimited and without boundaries, namely *anima*, to the bond of *anima*, to, and with, a containing, delimiting body. Then, the reverse: from sight to *vox* and *sound*, that is, from differentiated, contained "voice," which is particu-lar and identifiable, to auditory stuff, which is unlimited and uncon-tained. Chalcidius then takes up *silva*, and it is very interesting that he has come up with two words—*anima* and *silva*—to explain single the Greek word *hyle*. In the course of his translation and commentary, what is clear is that *silva* refers to and includes both that which is seen (all of the stuff of the world) as well as, and in full equivalence with, all of the *unseen* stuff of the world, or *anima*, that is, the unseen sub-stance of thoughts, memories, imaginations, and concepts. *Silva*, there-fore, includes, and is best exemplified by, sound. *All* stuff, seen and unseen, sounded and unsounded, is included in this disorderly thicket of material. One can then work with both in much the same way, as one shapes and differentiates thoughts in the same way that one fashions furniture from the material of the forest. Shaping, containing, and differentiating sound into discrete tones and joining them makes this whole question of dealing with unseen substance understandable.

The subject of *silva* is obviously Chalcidius's priority. This, summarized, is his thought-process. *Silva*, as we have noted, is the Greek *hyle* and encompasses everything made from "germane material" or "material germane to itself."[17] *Silva* also includes preexistent material and unseen substance, the Latin *anima*. So, *silva* can be viewed as piled up, disorderly, conceptual material as well as physical material, without delimitation and without boundaries, neither corporeal nor incorporeal.[18] *Silva* is foundational, but generated. In contrast to a quest for "origins," so common to a modern study of history, the time of generation or the concept of "beginning" is not very important, rather, "beginning" itself may not be a predominately temporal concept.[19] *Silva* is a composite, containing diverse properties and capacities.[20] *Silva*, then, as a simple mental picture is applicable to the entire physical and conceptual world. When divided up into individual *figurae* or individuated figures, one can imagine this individuation, or delineation, quite simply as a branch, the Latin *stirps* or *virga*, a protruding, defining stem from the disorderly mass of the entire forest of *silva*; as Chalcidius states, *stirps figurae*. The rough, heaped-up wood of a forest as an imaginary construct is placed before one's mind in terms of the careful separation of a single twig. Likewise, rough, undifferentiated conceptual substance containing inner energy can be bonded to a single written-out figure, a written "twig" or *virga*. The branch or twig is animated, both in the world we observe around us and conceptually as an indication of intention within the massive generality of sound.[21]

It is difficult to translate Greek into Latin. These difficulties prompted Chalcidius to explain his transformation of the concept. The result of his choice of this expression was that *silva*, for subsequent centuries, presented a substantial, material reality to the imagination of what was invisible, as well as conceptual. Chalcidius's translation of *hyle* into *silva*, rather than giving evidence for the poverty of the Latin language,[22] produced a very specific, guided, and useful outcome, namely, that unseen realities have, in fact, material properties and can be imagined or conceived exactly as one considers the visible, material, physical world at hand. In other words, one can work with, fashion, and bring out internal properties from conceptual material, placing pieces of concepts together, exactly as if one were building with blocks of wood. This gives a new seriousness to working with invisible, even inaudible, substance and brings to mind the question: do human beings ever take anything seriously that they cannot think of as "material" in nature?[23]

Furthermore, the term *silva* itself, for Chalcidius, is a collection—an entire repository or composite of modular, self-contained, identifiable significances. This is true for his readership—in fact, for ourselves—as well. *Silva* was available as preexistent substance and could be used as a resource. Indeed, incalculable use was made of this conceptual repository as writers through the centuries helped themselves, one after another, to this resource, chopping up manageable chunks of this forest, digging up blocks of conceptual substance, or separating out twigs or strands of concepts for their own use. The method is also clear in the case of Augustine, for whom an accent or pulse is a defined, delimited piece of enlivened substance—a "piece of life"—from the undifferentiated available mass of unseen, enlivened sound material, used by both speech and music.[24]

Martianus Capella is another example, as well as his 10th-century commentator Remigius of Auxerre, of an author who describes the entire repository of musical tones as a forest full of trees, the high ones giving off high tones, the lowest branches giving forth low tones. In an influential passage, Martianus Capella presents a forest full of trees with potentiality through their motions to produce high and low tones:

> Amidst these extraordinary scenes and these vicissitudes of Fortune, a sweet music arose from the trees, a melody arising from their contact as the breeze whispered through them; for the crests of the great trees were very tall, and because of this tension, reverberated with a sharp, high, sound; but whatever was close to and near the ground, with drooping boughs, shook with a deep heaviness of sound; while the trees of middle size in their contacts with each other sang together in fixed harmonies of the duple, and sesquialtera, the sesquitertia also, and even the semitones came between. So it happened that the forest poured forth, with melodious harmony, the whole music and song of the gods.[25]

Again, another indication of the influence of the *Timaeus*, and, especially, Chalcidius's translation, the term *silva*, within it, is Alfred the Great's use both of the term and concept within his introduction concerning the work of translation that he had undertaken in translating Augustine's *Soliloquies* from Latin into Anglo-Saxon. In a sense, the term *silva* itself is used as a resource. Alfred, in this context, brings out all of the concepts we have discussed, *silva, virga, via, via recta*—the forest, the twig, and finding a way through the forest, as well as the "chunks of the forest" used to build a commodious and useful house—a composition:

I then gathered for myself staves, and stud-shafts, and cross-beams, and belves for each of the tools that I could work with; and bow-timbers and bolt-timbers for every work that I could make—as many as I could carry of the comeliest trees. Nor came I home with a burden, for it pleased me not to bring all the wood home, even if I could bear it. In each tree I saw something that I needed at home; therefore I exhort every one who is able, and has many wains, to direct his steps to the self-same wood where I cut the stud-shafts. Let him there obtain more for himself, and load his wains with fair twigs, so that he may wind many a neat wall, and erect many a rare house, and build a fair enclosure, and therein dwell in joy and comfort both winter and summer, in such a manner as I have not yet done.

But He who taught me, and to whom the wood is pleasing, hath power to make me dwell more comfortably both in this transitory cottage by the road while I am on this world-pilgrimage, and also in the everlasting home which He hath promised us through Augustine and Jerome, and through many other Fathers, as I believe also for the merits of all those He will both make this way more convenient than it hitherto was, and especially will enlighten the eyes of my mind so that I may search out the right way to the eternal home, and to everlasting glory, and to eternal rest, which is promised us.

It is no wonder that one should labor in timber-work, both in the gathering and also in the building; but every man desireth that, after he hath built a cottage on his lord's lease and by his help, he may sometimes rest himself therein and go hunting, fowling, and fishing, and use it in every manner according to the lease, both on sea and land, until such time as he shall gain the fee-simple of the eternal heritage through his lord's mercy. So may the rich Giver do, who ruleth both these temporary cottages and the homes everlasting. May He who created both and ruleth both, grant me to be fit for each, both here to be useful, and thither to attain.[26]

As an example of the translational project, and the degrees of variation possible and taken, it is useful to compare another translation with the above (that is, Hargrove with Keynes-Lapidge):

I then gathered for myself staves and props and tie-shafts, and handles for each of the tools that I knew how to work with, and cross-bars and beams, and, for each of the structures which I knew how to build, the finest timbers I could carry. I never came away with a single load without wishing to bring home the whole of the forest, if I could have carried it all—in every tree I saw something for which I had a need at home. Accordingly, I would advise everyone who is strong and has many wagons to direct his steps to that same forest where I cut these props, and to fetch more for himself and to load his wagons with well-cut staves, so that he may weave many elegant walls and put up many splendid houses and so build a fine homestead, and there may live pleasantly and in tranquility both in winter and summer—as I have not yet done! But He who instructed me, to whom the forest was pleasing, may bring it about that I may abide more comfortably both in this temporary dwelling by this road as long as I am in this life, and also in the eternal home that He has promised us through the writings of St. Augustine and St. Gregory and St. Jerome, and through many other holy fathers: as I believe He will, through the merits of all these saints, both make this present road easier than it was before, and in particular will illuminate the eyes of my mind so that I can discover the most direct way to the eternal home and to eternal glory and to the eternal rest which is promised to us through those holy fathers. So may it be!

Nor is it any wonder that a man should work with such materials, both in transporting them and in building with them; but every man, when he has built a hamlet on land leased to him by his lord and with his lord's help, likes to stay there some time, and go hunting, fowling and fishing and to employ himself in every way on that leased land, both on sea and land, until the time when he shall deserve bookland and a perpetual inheritance through his lord's kindness. May the bounteous benefactor, who rules both these temporary habitations as well as those eternal abodes, so grant! May He who created both and rules over both grant that I be fit for both: both to be useful here and likewise to arrive there.

Alfred's preface clearly, and I believe, quite consciously, brings to the fore all of the mental pictures with which we have been dealing, and which are inherent within Chalcidius's translational choice, namely: *silva* (wood), useful, collected together, and selected (Alfred states that he did not bring all of the wood home with him); branches or twigs (*stirps virgae*) as differentiated from the general store of wood available; mode, manner, way of proceeding (*modus in viam*), a way of moving through the thicket of the wood, and, by implication, of life; as well as Alfred's own conceptualization of his mental work as imaginable in the highly concrete, substantial, and practical terms of gathering, cutting, appropriating useful wood from the thicket of available material within the forest. Further, in this passage, there is a constant shift between practical, concrete labor with wood in the forest and mental, conceptual, compositional work with the mind and with unseen *materia*.

It is not impossible that Alfred actually had read Chalcidius's translation of, with its extensive commentary on, Plato's *Timaeus*. We do not know this for sure. But whether or not this is true, by the time of Alfred's writing, the concept of both visible and invisible *materia/substantia* as a forest (*silva*) to be worked with as one worked with wood had infiltrated the mental world in which Alfred lived, and the concept of *silva* was reinforced as well by what he could see around him—hence the power of this Chalcidius's choice of term.[27]

Finally, we return to Dante, as he writes in his introduction to the *Inferno* of the *Divine Comedy*:

> When in the midst of my *course* of life,
> I found myself in a dark, opaque *forest*,
> And found that I had lost my *way* . . .
> (Nel mezzo del cammin de nostra vita
> mi ritrovai per una selva oscura
> che la diritta via era smarrita . . .)[28]

But the final question here, also to be answered more completely in the chapters that follow, is how medieval writers indeed took Chalcidius at his word, namely, that music as a material and measurement discipline also clearly exemplified concepts and terms contained within the *Timaeus latinus*, as well as within Chalcidius's commentary. Chalcidius stated that music provided a link between abstraction and physical, sensorially perceived exemplification. Writers on music for the next millennium essentially provided anthologies of examples for this background, as we will see, but here, at least, are three of them. First, perhaps most strikingly, music notation (*figurae*) itself is literally a twig, *stirps, virga*, indicating an individual *tonus*, within the general, inchoate mass of possible sonic material, or *silva*. The *virga* as basis for delineating sound is discussed. Secondly, an extension of this concept of twig, enlivened branch, or stem is, as Chalcidius's commentary points out in many contexts, a *figura*. Whether of letter, of number, or music, notational *figura*, all use the same Latin word, *figura*, to bring up specific properties such as movement, color, individuality delineated from the congested mass of material. The *figurae* contained within this 11th-century manuscript (see Example IX), now in the Paris National Library, bring all of these attributes of delineated, animated *figurae* together with the *modi* of musical motion. Properties such as motion or gesture, color, position, demeanor, and instruments delineate individuality from the mass of aggregated material. Chalcidius has a great deal to say, not only, as we have noted, about *silva*, but also concerning *figurae* as differentiating agents or instruments of delineation. *Figurae* are made, that is, carefully constructed with a purpose in mind, hence, they delineate by connected lines, as well as by recognizable shape within material. They are fashioned in order to give forth the properties of that material, hence, a *figura*, itself is an instrument within material for the purpose of delineating individuality within conglomerated reality, making both the intention of the illustrator clear as well as the internal properties of the illustrated.[29]

Thirdly, from many expressions within the Latin *Timaeus* that were drawn into service as a vocabulary both to address music, as well as use music as an example of what was at stake, one can be chosen from many expressions that made their way through a network of centers of teaching and learning, particularly in the 11th and 12th centuries. *Fabricator mundi* occurs in several contexts, for example, early on in the Latin *Timaeus*, for example, *"cur rerum conditor fabricatorque"* (the maker, "fabricator" of all things)[30] marks out the influence of the *Timaeus*, particularly within the liturgical books used by, and within, cathedral school environments, such as that of 12th-century Nevers. (We have already considered in detail an entire liturgical celebration from this cathedral.) Expressions that evidence relationship to, and cognizance of, the *Timaeus* are plentiful, not only within treatises concerning music, its properties and function as a discipline, but also connected to music that was an integral part of daily life in terms of the series of ritualized, liturgical events that gave order and sense to the course of the day. It is more than coincidence that the texted Responsory *Fabricator mundi* can be found so frequently in manuscripts of the office hours (which occur every three hours throughout the day at a monastery or cathedral).

The *melisma, Fabrice mundi*, with several alternative texts, *Facinora nostra, Facture dominans*, occurs for many centuries within the early morning office hours. (See Editions: Music to Sing.) The *Timaeus latinus* provides a vocabulary for describing music, and as Chalcidius's commentary, as well as the context of his explanation of *silva*, makes clear, music made basic principles such as *silva*, as well as *silva*'s individuation into branches, stems, or *virgae*, plain.

How did music do this? One is amazed, since the answer is at once too simple, and on the other hand, hard to place in perspective. By the materials it used—sound and time—music itself demonstrated Chalcidius's priority, as well as his most important contribution to such a far-reaching topic of the substance of the world, both visible and invisible. Sonorous substance is massive and undifferentiated, but it can become delineated by means of internal, germane properties of music material, that is, through motion and time. Sound is unseen, yet real; movement is inherent within sound, as in all material. So, the principal point of *silva*, the equivalence of material substance as both seen and unseen and the ultimate reality of both, are all demonstrated most clearly within music. Likewise, mind/spirit (*anima*) is considered to be a substantial reality. Music as well is unseen, yet palpable, material reality, and displays all of the properties of material, in that one can become satiated with musical substance, and it is, as well, addictive.

Such, also, was the power of Chalcidius's translational metaphor that even in the 19th century, *silva*, or a "forest full of trees," constitutes a repository of sonorous material to be accessed by the composer of the musical work. The overture to Carl Maria von Weber's early 19th-century opera *Der Freischütz*, for example, begins in the forest with diffused, sonorous material that is then selected and developed, strand by strand, in the course of the opera. Stage-sets that have been recovered from the early 19th century also often bring the forest to the fore. *Silva*, exemplified by music, turns up again in the 19th century—a dark forest full of trees, an undifferentiated mass of material, with generative potential for discovery, realization, and perfection. *Silva*—the forest—is preexistent, from whence melodies of the opera that follows are differentiated.

From the forest, then, of limitless material, emphasized by Chalcidius in his Latin translation of Plato's *Timaeus*, we move to other components of a medieval mental world in which music made difficult concepts plain.

NOTES

1. See the selection of manuscripts brought together for Waszink's edition of the *Timaeus latinus*, pp. CVI–XXXI (see note 7), which includes sources from the entire continent of Latinized Europe from the 9th to the 15th centuries. It provides an astonishing array of witnesses to the dissemination and unquestioned importance of the *Timaeus latinus* and evidence for the presence of the *Timaeus* in its Latin translation very early in the Middle Ages, for example at St. Amand in northern France, from where the ninth-century writer on music as a discipline, Hucbald, hailed, and in Anglo-Saxon England. Surprisingly, the Latin translation of the *Timaeus* with its commentary has been neglected, as Peter Dronke, in his recent study of the *Timaeus* also points out. See *The Spell of Calcidius: Platonic Concepts and Images in the Medieval West* (Florence, 2008), especially *silva*, pp. 25–30.

2. We are dealing with the Latin translation of the Greek *Timaeus*, therefore, the Latin expressions as Chalcidius's choices should be taken into consideration, rather than what one might assume to be English equivalent expressions. Words are important. Languages are in many ways both incommensurable, even incompatible; and historical changes that deal mainly with concepts frequently divide medieval Latin words from their recognizable English cognates. These cognates, such as "figure," "mode," "trope," or "harmony" also have lost their pungency and specificity through overuse that has in some cases rendered them nearly meaningless. Due to the subject at hand, the translation of one Latin term, *silva*, this chapter will also discuss the translational process itself, since translation is such an important aspect of medieval mental culture.

3. Plato, *Timaeus,* in *Collected Works IX,* trans. R. G. Bury, Loeb Classical Library (Cambridge, MA, 1929, repr. 1942, 1952, 1961, 1966, 1975, 1981]), p. 49. The edition in use today (1981) reflects priorities and choices of terms of the late 1920s (1929).

4. Raymond Klibansky, *The Continuity of the Platonic Tradition: Plato's Parmenides in the Middle Ages* (London, 1939, repr. 1982, 1984), p. 28. Discussing the translations of Plato's *Meno* and *Phaedo* in the mid-12th century, Klibansky writes: "The importance of these works, however, cannot be compared with that of the *Timaeus.* This dialogue, or rather its first part, was studied and quoted throughout the Middle Ages, and there was hardly a mediaeval library of any standing which had not a copy of Chalcidius' version and sometimes also a copy of the fragment translated by Cicero. Although these facts are well known, their significance for the history of ideas has perhaps not been sufficiently grasped by historians." Klibansky's statement is even more true for an assessment of music writing within the discipline of music throughout the Middle Ages. It should be mentioned in this context that the copy that was believed to be the oldest extant manuscript of the *Timaeus latinus* was that of Hucbald of St. Amand, who also wrote at least one treatise on music, and even in the 12th century continued to enjoy a reputation for having served as a consultant for the establishment of *scholae cantorum*—singing schools that were always attached to schools that also enjoyed reputations as centers of medieval learning, as, apparently, the cathedral school at Nevers in the late 11th, early 12th centuries (see van Deusen, *Music at Nevers Cathedral: Principal Sources of Medieval Chant,* 2 vols. [Binningen, Switzerland, 1980], especially the introduction to vol. 1). The link between the *Timaeus* and utterly basic music conceptualizations with attendant vocabulary has not, in view of its importance, come under investigation.

5. See, for example, Klaus Schroer and Klaus Irle, ". . . *Ich aber quadrere den Kreis . . ." Leonardo da Vincis Proportionsstudie* (Münster, 1998).

6. The importance of the *Timaeus latinus* not only was not sufficiently recognized in 1939, when Klibansky noted that fact, but continues to be almost completely ignored, as is the case in Thomas J. Mathiesen's recent book on Greek writers on music in antiquity and the Middle Ages, *Apollo's Lyre. Greek Music and Music Theory in Antiquity and the Middle Ages* (Lincoln, NE, 1999). The writer was apparently unaware that an edition of the *Timaeus,* with a valuable introduction to the translation and commentary, as well as important indices, had appeared since Johannes Wrobel's 19th-century edition. If Professor Mathiesen had seen the indices pointing to both sources accessed by Chalcidius, as well as the influence upon a Latin readership during the entire medieval period, he, no doubt, would not have been so dismissive of the work as "largely derivative" (p. 616), nor treated it so cursorily, as if Chalcidius's *Timaeus* was scarcely worth considering, even by mention. Further, Bernice Kaczynski in her "Translations: Latin and Greek," in *Medieval Latin: An Introduction and Bibliographical Guide,* eds. F. A. C. Mantello and A. G. Rigg (Washington, D.C., 1996), pp. 718–722, makes no mention of what was, probably, next to Jerome's translation of the Bible, the most influential translation of the Middle Ages. Another point should be made here, namely, that the

transmission of the Latin *Timaeus*, as well as the later, 12th-century translations of the *Meno* and *Phaedo* are difficult to access, since, unlike the transmission of key phrases to be found, for example, in the *Metaphysics* or *Physics*
of Aristotle, Plato is more difficult to quote, hence, identify, due to both the
structure and content of his arguments. Plato's influence must therefore be in-
ferred, but there are good reasons for these inferences.

7. cf. Waszink's edition: 61.6, 145.4, 259.5, 286.14, 325.22 (*Timaeus a Calcidio translatus commentarioque instructus*, ed. J. H. Waszink [Plato latinus, IV, ed.
Raymond Klibansky, London, Leiden, 1975], hereafter referred to as edition
[ed.]).

8. ed. 273.15–16.

9. ed. 167.6, to be expanded upon in the more extended section of Chalcidius's commentary, 268–354.

10. See Mary Carruthers, *The Craft of Thought: Meditation, Rhetoric, and the
Making of Images, 400–1200* (Cambridge, 1998), who writes of imaginative
"tools" and regards them primarily as rhetorical (as they also are) but does
not discuss the fundamentally material nature of what she describes.

11. See also the *Metaphysica*, I.3,983b. An earlier study of this concept can
be found in van Deusen, "The Problem of Matter, the Nature of Mode, and the
Example of Melody in Medieval Music Writing," in *The Harp and the Soul: Essays in Medieval Music* (Lewiston, NY, 1989), pp. 1–45.

12. Cf. ed. Waszink introduction, xxvii, with regard to the passage quoted
above (c. 268): Necessitatem porro nunc appellat hylen, quam nos Latine silvam possumus nominare, the reader is drawn to the comment of van Winden,
p. 23: . . ." therefore, Calcidius' lengthy chapter on *materia/silva* is actually
more than a treatment of one of the two principal subjects . . . It is, in point of
fact the fundamental part of his entire commentary." Cf. J.C.M. van Winden,
Calcidius on Matter, His Doctrine and Sources (Leiden, 1959).

13. This subject of "things that are no longer present" is taken up in detail
in the *Phaedo*, which became known to the Latin-reading public in the mid-
12th century. By the beginning of the 14th century, it could be found in major
emerging libraries, such as what would become the Vatican and the Sorbonne.
See van Deusen, "The Harp and the Soul: The Image of the Harp and Trecento
Reception of Plato's *Phaedo*," in *The Harp and the Soul*, pp. 384–416, especially
pp. 388ff.

14. I have deliberately avoided the implications of this entire terminologi-
cal nexus of *harmonia*, also for the reason that Stephen Gersh has thoroughly
treated it, with important implications for analysis, not only for the terms
under consideration, but generally. See Stephen Gersh's pivotal *Concord in
Discourse: Harmonics and Semiotics in Late Classical and Early Medieval Platonism*
(Berlin, 1996), especially his consideration of Chalcidius and the *Timaeus Latinus* (pp. 128–139, 148–149). The implication here is that if you truly understood *harmonia* as exemplified in the successful use of tones, using the material
of sound that is unseen, you understood, as well, what holds the world, as
well as the human body, together.

15. The Latin text has been included here in order to select and recognize
the actual Latin words, which we have discussed and which have cognates in

the English language (ed. c 297, p. 272). Note the use of *per vocem. ex musica. harmonia, harmonicam animam, in superioribus, naturalemque, rhythmis modisque* (a source of the concept of "rhythmic modes"), *immodulatas, in musica, vulgus delectatur, a ratione atque intellegentia separetur, animas a via recta, ad symphoniam.* Most of the priorities of writing concerning music are included in this passage:

> Quantumque per vocem utilitatis capitur ex musica, totum hoc constat hominum generi propter harmonia tributum, quia iuxta rationem harmonicam animam in superioribus aedificaverat naturalemque eius actum rhythmis modisque constare dixerat, sed haec exolescere animae ob consortium corporis necessario obtinente oblivione proptereaque immodulatas fore animas plurimorum. Medelam huius vitii dicit esse in musica positam, non in ea qua vulgus delectatur quaeque ad voluptatem facta excitat vitia non numquam, sed in illa divina quae numquam a ratione atque intellegentia separetur; hanc enim censet exorbitantes animas a via recta revocare demum ad symphoniam veterem.

> *Cf. Augustine, De musica, who, in his own words, says the same (PL 32), also articles, "Music," "Rhythm," in Augustine through the Ages: An Encyclopedia, ed. Allan D. Fitzgerald, O.S.A. (Grand Rapids, Michigan, 1999).*

16. The passage quoted and paraphrased in English above continues:

> Optima porro symphonia est in moribus nostris iustitia, virtutum omnium principalis, per quam ceterae quoque virtutes suum munus atque opus exequuntur, ut ratio quidem dux sit, vigor vero intimus, qui est iracundiae similis, auxiliatorem se rationi volens praebeat; porro haec provenire sine modulatione non possunt, modulatio demum sine symphonia nulla sit, ipsa symphonia sequitur musicam. Procul dubio musica exornat animam rationabiliter ad antiquam naturam revocans et efficiens talem demum, qualem initio deus opifex eam fecerat. Tota porro musica in voce et auditu et sonis posita est. Utilis ergo etiam iste sensus est philosophiae totius assecutioni ad notationem intellegibilis rei. (c. 267, pp. 272–273)

17. Cf. c. 268, pp. 273–274. Chalcidius not only invests his commentary with his own interpretations—the obvious bases, in any case, for a commentary—but the translation of Plato's text is informed by this conceptualization as well, as for example, his emphasis on the concept/word *fabricator* (see also Edition III) *fabricatus* est, which brings up concrete, material connotations. See, for example, 36 D (p. 28): "Unam quippe, ut erat, eam et indivisam reliquit, interiorem vero scidit sexies septemque impares orbes fabricatus est iuxta dupli et tripli spatia orbesque ipsos contraria ferri iussit agitatione, ex quibus septem tres quidem pari velocitate, quattuor vero et sibimet ipsis et ad comparationem ceterorum impari dissimilique sed cum ratione motu." Note again Latin expressions (which also have cognates in English) that we have previously encountered.

18. ed. c. 272 (p.276): "Quippe primum elementum universae rei silva est informis ac sine qualitate quam, ut sit mundus, format intellegibilis species; ex quibus, silva videlicet et specie . . . with editor's note to Augustine's *De Genesi ad litteram*, I 4, 9: silva informis ac sine qualitate . . ."

19. ed. c.276. [p. 280].

20. Cf. ed. c. 274 (pp. 278f): "longe tamen difficilius declarare ac docere." The bringing out of a "work into the light of day" is both difficult to

accomplish, and difficult to teach, a statement with which most of us would agree.

21. In other words, *silva* as *fundamentum* is differentiated into *figurae, figuratis* (also Aristotle, *Metaphysica*, A4, 985b14); *hyle* differentiated into *schema* (also Aristotle, *Physica* A 2, 184b2). *Silva,* therefore, is more than a "congestion" but, rather, limitless resource.

22. Peter Green makes the point that since educated Romans were thoroughly bilingual in Greek and Latin, that the translation, rather than giving the only access to a Greek text, was regarded as an interpretation of that text— a Greek original that was fully accessible as well to the reader. See Green, *Classical Bearings: Interpreting Ancient History and Culture* (Berkeley, Los Angeles, 1989), pp. 264–265. Further, Green argues that free, not "literal," translation has been in and out of fashion at all times (p. 266), while missing the point. It is impossible to avoid translating what it is that one wishes to communicate into one's translation, a translation being a metaphor (*translatio*) for the view one holds, whether one articulates these views to oneself or not.

23. For the linguistic properties discussed in this section, see A. L. Becker, *Beyond Translation* (Ann Arbor, MI, 1995). The assertion made at least more than once that Chalcidius received his concept of *silva* from "the Pythagoreans" either contradicts nearly everything Pythagoras is credited for originating, or has little to do directly with what Pythagoras supposedly advocated, that is, the immortality and transmigration of souls, and that the soul is made of air. (Cf. the concise account of Richard D. McKirahan, Jr., *Philosophy Before Socrates: An Introduction with Texts and Commentary* [Indianapolis/Cambridge, 1994], pp. 79–115.) Furthermore, the problem of *silva* is not only conceptual but translational, having to do with specific languages and linguistic propensities, potentialities, and properties. See also Stephen Gersh's valuable discussion of the concept of "structure," especially in chapter l of *Concord in Discourse.*

24. Cf. article on Augustine's *De musica* in *Augustine, an Encyclopedia.*

25. *Martianus Capella and the Seven Liberal Arts,* English translation, William H. Stahl and Richard Johnson with E. L. Burge (New York, 1977), vol. 2, 9f: every allusion finds exemplification within the medieval discipline of music, as, for example, a quotation, for the most part, from Remigius of Auxerre's commentary on the cited passage in Regino of Prüm's treatise: "Quicquid vero terrae confine et propinquum fuerat, rami videlicet inclinatiores et humiliores ac terrae viciniores quatiebat, id est, impellebat, repercutiebat rauca gravitas. At media, id est mediae partes ipsius silvae, coniuncta sibi spatia concinebant duplis succentibus" (cf. Gerbert, *Scriptores de musica* [GS], I, 234 with Remigius of Auxerre's Commentary on *The Marriage of Philology and Mercury,* ed. Cora E. Lutz [Leiden, 1962–65], I:86f). See also van Deusen, "The Problem of Matter, the Nature of Mode, and the Example of Melody in Medieval Music Writing," in *The Harp and the Soul,* pp. 1–45, especially pp. 6–7. Unlike Martianus, Macrobius, in his *Commentary on the Dream of Scipio* (English translation, William Harris Stahl [New York, 1952]) does not emphasize *silva.* See, for example, book I, chapter 5, proceeding with Cicero's Dream: "What is this great and pleasing sound that fills my ears," answered by "that is a concord of tones separated by unequal but nevertheless carefully propositioned intervals . . . . The high and low tones blended together produce different

harmonies." Macrobius writes of metallic bodies that are not subject to a state of flux, not perfect but solid (*nasta*) (p. 95); and the demarcation between water and air as harmony, that is, a compatible and harmonious union, as an interval uniting lower with upper, reconciling incongruent factors (p. 107). It is of further interest that in the west Frankish territory, now France, shortly following the writing of both Remigius's commentary as well as Regino's treatise, *figurae* of music notation evidence relationship between relative spatial highness and lowness on a manuscript page and highness or lowness of actual pitch, a relationship taken for granted today, but which was not common in eastern Frankish manuscripts until several centuries later. A further observation: just as Chalcidius apparently chose an emphasis in his Latin term *silva*, so also Latin medieval writers later on in the 12th century appear to choose *silva*—or not. Bernardus Silvestris does, cf. Brian Stock, *Myth and Science in the Twelfth Century. A Study of Bernard Silvester* (Princeton, 1972), pp. 35, 67, also note, 69, 70, 77n. 84, 87, 97–118, 119, 121, 122, 134, 138, 143n, 199n, 203n, 222, 226, 233; a study in itself. William of Conches in his commentary on the *Timaeus* avoids the term altogether, using *materia* instead of *silva*.

26. See *King Alfred's Old English Version of St. Augustine's Soliloquies,* trans. Hargrove, pp. 1–2; which has been included here with that of Simon Keynes and Michael Lapidge, in *Alfred the Great: Asser's Life of King Alfred and Other Contemporary Sources* (Harmondsworth, UK/New York, 1983), pp. 138–139, based on the Anglo-Saxon edition of T. A. Carnicelli (Cambridge, MA, 1969), pp. 47–48. See also Janet Bately's article, "The Nature of Old English Prose," in *The Cambridge Companion to Old English Literature,* eds. Malcolm Godden and Michael Lapidge (Cambridge, UK, 1991), p. 77:

> Alfred's reworking of his Latin sources in the *Boethius* and the *Soliloquies* is indeed considerable. At times it seems as though he is using his Latin texts as no more than a spring-board for his own considered responses to their contents and his personal interests. (His own fine extended metaphor, in the preface to the *Soliloquies*, is of the would-be builder who goes to the forest—that is, the writings of the church fathers—for materials.) The freedom that he takes with his authorities is too considerable to be dealt with in detail here.

See also Christine Fell's article "Perceptions of Transience," in *The Cambridge Companion to Old English Literature,* in which a portion of this passage is given as an example of Alfred's understanding of the paired concepts of transience and eternity. Fell then compares Carnicelli's edition of the Anglo-Saxon text with Alfred's version of St. Augustine's *Soliloquies* (p. 173). Translators, editors, as well as commentators have all brought out their own priorities with the emphasis, based directly on the Anglo-Saxon version, in the Keynes-Lapidge translation, on *forest (ontimber)*. Alfred's translation of Augustine's *Soliloquies* survives in a single manuscript, now British Library, Cotton Vitellius A.xv, ff. 4–59, mid-12th-century, unknown origin, cf. Keynes and Lapidge, *Alfred the Great,* p. 299. An edition of the Anglo-Saxon text is included in Carnicelli, pp. 47–48.

27. Michael Lapidge has stated that there is little evidence for libraries owned by Anglo-Saxon kings, but it would seem that King Alfred, based on

his translating projects, "most presumably had assembled a royal library" of some distinction. The cluster of pointed references Alfred makes to the forest full of material substantiates Chalcidius's priority and provides clues as well both to Alfred's educational background as well as to the landscape of his own learning. Cf. Michael Lapidge, "Surviving Booklists from Anglo-Saxon England," in Michael Lapidge and Helmut Gneuss, ed., *Learning and Literature in Anglo-Saxon England: Studies Presented to Peter Clemoes on the Occasion of his Sixty-Fifth Birthday* (Cambridge, UK, 1985), p. 34n.

28. *The Divine Comedy of Dante Alighieri: Inferno,* Italian text with translation, Allen Mandelbaum (Berkeley, Los Angeles, 1980, repr. New York, 1982), cf. commentary, p. 344: the commentator concentrates his remarks on "darkness," rather than "forest" (*selva*). Other modern languages also retain both the term and the significance, such as Hungarian: *szil* (tree), *szilánk* (splinter), *szilárd* (firm, solid, massive), *szilfa* (a wood, not only visible, but an invisible aggregated mass). *Sz* in Hungarian is pronounced as the *s* in English. But the topic of *in via recta*, the "right way" through an undifferentiated "mass of material" is relevant today, as, for example, Melanie Mitchell's *Complexity. A Guided Tour* (Oxford, 2009).

29. Chalcidius's *figurae* are plain (ed. p. 61); they demonstrate (ed. p. 62); they are composed of lines (ed. pp. 69, 88); they have properties (ed. p. 305); and they are composed, or fictive. Upon this basis, that is, of the delineatory potentiality of the concept of *figura*, Chalcidius summarizes the system of disciplines that delineate particularity, connection, and motion, namely, grammar-arithmetic, logic-geometry, and rhetoric-physics.

30. *Timaeus* ed. p. 22 Cf. p. 23: for the wider context: ad cuius animantis similitudinem constituerit eum suus conditor (*conditor*; fashioner, fabricator).

6

"They All Read the Same Books": A Book-Bag from Antiquity

What, then, were these "medieval people" reading? The books they read, the questions they raised, and the answers they received—and were willing to accept—are all important issues to explore. Some of their conclusions were not definitive—in some cases, the conclusion was, there was none. In any case their wits were sharpened by dialogue, as are ours. These issues remain topics today. Far from a musty museum full of decaying, useless, irrelevant tools, the topics to be considered here, finding exemplification in musical properties as well as composition, are still at the forefront of the modern sciences such as physics, biology, psychology, and education, as well, certainly, as philosophy.

We bring out a book-bag from what is commonly known as Latin antiquity: Chalcidius's translation of Plato's *Timaeus*, treating available *materia*, was discussed in detail in the preceding chapter. In addition, Virgil's *Aeneid* has been mentioned briefly, but with the respect it deserves, since every literate medieval school-child no doubt knew large portions of the *Aeneid* by memory. Cicero's treatise concerning the nature of the gods, dealing again, as the *Timaeus*, with *materia/substantia/natura*; as well as what Quintilian, in his books on rhetoric, made of Cicero, fashioning what was to the imagination—the inner eye—a living mentor out of the great orator's own quotations. All these texts have come into the consideration of components within a medieval mental environment. These are components, but we are also considering resources for actual use in every situation. The writings of all of these authors—and several more—together constitute the *silva*, or repository, of preexistent *materia* to be used at will and according to the expertise of the user—material that was there, available for the using. We have mentioned Martianus Capella's *Marriage of Philology and Mercury* as presenting connections between voice and content, between communication and object; giving system and rationality to an organized program of education that included the study of *particular* sounds or things, *relationships* between words or lines, and *movement* between words or physical bodies; leading, then, to thought, memory, and concept as invisible substance. All of these works deal with a nexus of ideas as well as a progression from "raw" material to consciously differentiated and meaningful outline or shape that could indicate individual properties within that material on to the properties themselves within this material, such as movement, transformation, mutation, and degeneration, as well as actualization. How does one communicate all of this in a resourceful, interesting, cogent, and persuasive manner? That must be learned too. Making the connection, or *copula,* between communication and what was being communicated was a task in itself.

But the Bible, as an immense thicket (as it is described in the Middle Ages), was considered a huge quarry, a resource without limitation, a great, "opaque," and vast forest full of expressions of inner and outer states, apt phrases, trenchant vocabulary useful in every possible situation, individual personalities, as well as groups, narratives, historical situations, needful advice, examples of good conduct (as well as for the contrary—in order to deter and discourage unproductive behavior), predictions of the future, songs, hymns, and laments. All this, and much more as well. The Bible is filled with a multiplicity of genres, of patterns for use: within the Bible, both "stuff" and the necessary models for using this stuff are available. A medieval writer, reader, or composer could, in other words, cut up content and make it one's own, appropriate it, digest it, as was also pointed out by medieval teachers. And this is exactly what happened. To appropriate, connect, and use material, especially from the Book of Psalms, as we have seen, underlies medieval mental culture.

The Bible, then, was considered preexistent stuff, already "there," available to use. One could also take vigorous issue with the Bible, adding one's own commentary, chunk by chunk, or line by line, interacting with the topics, directions, outcomes, and perceived conclusions, or take issue with those who, through the centuries, had gone before. The Bible, again, particularly the Psalms, was a shared capital, a possession held in common, as the Psalms were sung in their entirety weekly, from beginning to end, and as they were disengaged from their familiar place within the Book of Psalms in order to give emphasis to a specific theme, with its accompanying *figura,* as this theme would have been appropriate for a specific day (such as, the Epiphany or the Celebration of the Three Kings).

Not only were the combined books of the Bible a preexistent re-source for daily use, but the Bible in all of its dimensions articulated the most basic principles of life itself, namely, dimensions of the "stuff of life," that is, time. Event by event, moving forward in incremental steps, large and small, some of the books of the Bible, such as the his-torical books of the accounts of the kings of Israel and Judah, Chron-icles, the Books of Samuel, and Judges, present time as it is lived in the world, in that one thing follows another. There is a predictable se-quence of before and after, prior and posterior. But, simultaneously, one is made aware of other times; there are other alternative ways of moving and experiencing time: a simultaneity of times, so to speak. This overlap of simultaneous times is borne out again with the Psalms, but also in the prophetic books such as Isaiah, Jeremiah, and especially Daniel. All of these concepts of time, such as the concepts of prior and posterior, are elementary tools of intellection, but important nonethe-less. We use these tools constantly when we read, more often intui-tively rather than consciously, articulating to ourselves what we are doing—with what understanding, or "mode," we are using to "move" through a passage that we are reading.

The Bible also provided models for individual composition taken up throughout the Middle Ages. There are models for narration, for episodic continuity in the Pentateuch, with books such as Genesis, Ex-odus, Deuteronomy, or, in the New Testament, the Acts of the Apos-tles, giving a concept of a genre to medieval writers of the lives of saints.[1] The prophet Jeremiah, and especially the Book of Lamenta-tions, as well as King David's lament for his son Absalom (in 2 Sam-uel), offered a model of the lament, or medieval *planctus,* the *deploration.* There were models for love songs (The Songs of Solomon, or "Song of Songs"), models for praise (in the Psalms), and models for lyric expres-sion (interspersed throughout the scriptures, and, especially, again, in the Psalms). These models provided more than just patterns to be fol-lowed, rather, they were considered to be made up of a preexistent substance that was available for use. They invited interaction and gave encouragement as a place to begin one's own composition.

A good deal of what was contained within the scriptures, however, was not always clear and apparent. The sheer opacity of the scriptures made for some confusion. The panorama of themes made for a welter of varied and diverse *figurae.* Difficulties were compensated by inte-rior growth, in terms of greater attention to details—the result of ever more careful reading or listening. Further, one made logical progress in terms of following a thought to its conclusion, as well as obtain-ing a wider grasp of experience than one perhaps might be able to achieve in one's own environment, both in terms of the past as well as the world at large. Understandably, therefore, the Bible was the single most truly indispensable textbook for medieval schools; there was no separation between "sacred" and "secular," as is common today. The study of the Bible was useful for the training of sophisticated and useful mental habits, as well as providing topics for discussion and individual interpretation.

Perhaps the most important intellectual tool that the study of the Bible encouraged was that of interpretation, expressed as *modi*—modes of signifying, of articulating—and making available inherent properties of the material at hand. This is one of the most important considerations of the Middle Ages as we have seen. The sheer mass of speech or sound within the biblical scriptures, consisting of vowels and consonants, could be indicated by the *figurae* of letters within the alphabet. It was repeatedly noticed that certain characteristic ways or manners of working with this material of speech appeared to delineate, differentiate, place emphasis upon, and provide directionality, so that within a general mass of sound substance, differences (*differentiae*) became clear. Emphasis, turns of phrases, and other characteristic gestures indicate whether a statement signifies the intention to give forth a historical, indicative "fact" to be received literally; projects an allegory to be wrestled with, which, in fact, has an intention differing considerably from its external *figurae* arranged in words themselves; has a tropological message or an action mandate, indicating by means, most frequently, of a metaphor, that is, an action to be taken or imitated; or refers to future events to be considered and imagined. These—the historical or literal, allegorical, tropological or analogical, and eschatological or anagogical modes—were, as we have seen, the modes of verbal interpretation available to medieval educators, since they can be found and identified in countless situations within the Bible.[2] As readers alternated within the books of the Bible, so these modes alternated with one another when used with music tones throughout the mass and office-hour celebrations of a day such the Epiphany.

The impact of the study and interpretation of the Bible can be seen in its impact upon medieval *cantus,* which later expressed what Augustine had written: "When a song, or cantus, is sung, the sound is heard simultaneously. It is not diffuse, chaotic sound that comes first, and then is shaped into song." This constitutive process takes place instantaneously, simultaneously on two levels, that is, the shaping of sound into characteristic, recognizable, musical intervals indicative of a certain mode of meaning, and the shaping of words into characteristic phrases that also indicate a mode of meaning. This happens simultaneously, as meaning is perceived simultaneously with the sound of words as they are read aloud. In comparing the Mass for the Lenten season of the church year with the Proper of the Mass, dealing with particular occasions (see Editions: Music to Sing), it is clear that the different parts of the day appear to use the same general music material; but repetition and gesture, in other words, certain characteristics or *figurae*, indicate differing modes or manners of moving through the same sound substance. Whether one is capable of reading music or not, this difference is clear from the visual images of "pieces of sound" (single tones) on the page.

The same is true textually in that essentially the same words are used—quite normal words of the Latin language—but external gestures, repetitions, characteristic turns of phrases indicate, as well, a textual mode of interpretation. This simultaneity and constant alternation of four musical *manneriae* and four textual interpretational senses or modes, takes place whenever music and text come together and unite syllable and tone in a particular, one could even say, intimate, way. During the course of the mass celebration, all of the musical modes are given expression, as well as all of the interpretatory verbal modes, in a constant alternation, or *alternatim*, procedure. An important result of this is that *all* of the musical and textual parts of the mass are necessary, as, for example, the tropes, which are tropological, that is, which provide analogies in terms of containing an action mandate to be obeyed (as the mandate, "praise" with the indicative *figurae*: *laudate, psallite*). Sequences, too, begin with the allegorical mode of textual interpretation and conclude with a clear eschatological close, presenting a particularly good example of *alternatim*, since they are then followed by the historical textual mode of the gospel reading (see Edition IV). The points to be taken here are: (a) The constructional principles of the Bible influenced medieval intellectual culture. (b) The mass celebration during the Middle Ages when it contained tropes and sequences presented an entire complete modal system. (c) The concept of *alternatim*, taken from the alternation of texts within the Bible, is based on the fact that, just as the texts of scripture alternate the four modes of scriptural interpretation, the historical, allegorical, tropological, and eschatological, so likewise the order of events within the mass ceremony simultaneously alternates the four *manneriae* of musical modes with the four modes of scriptural interpretation.

"Modes," then, are neither abstract nor strictly classificatory. Rather, this system of alternating modes expresses the material at hand, that is, in terms of tone and speech. This is an important, though difficult, point. Again, Augustine, in the *Confessions* (which parallels the alternating emotional states of the Psalms), makes a point of the fact that from a material, many and diverse interpretations can result. He writes, in the context of the command "increase and multiply," which was biblically made, as he notes, to persons, not animals:

> In all these things, we find multitudes and abundances and increases. But only in *figurae* given corporeal expression and in intellectual concepts do we find an increasing and multiplying which illustrate how one thing can be expressed in several ways (*modi*), and how one formulation can bear many meanings. Figures given corporeal expressions are the creatures generated from the waters, necessary because of our deep involvement in those things that are seen. But because of the fertility of reason, I interpret the generation of humanity to signify the generation of concepts [showing here an equation made between seen, fleshly *materia* and conceptual *materia*]. That is why we believe that you, Lord, addressed both seen and invisible in the words "increase and multiply." By this blessing we understand you to grant us the capacity and ability to articulate in many ways [*manneriae*] what we hold to be a single concept, and to give a plurality of meanings to a single text that we might read. It is said "the waters of the sea are filled," because their movement means the variety of significations. Likewise the earth is filled with human offspring. Its dryness shows itself in human energy, and the mastery of it by reason.[3]

Let us focus on three aspects here. First, as we have noticed, there is a proportional relationship between seen and unseen substance. This equivalence is crucial to the Latin translation of Plato's *Timaeus*, as we have discussed. Secondly, Augustine has used passages from the Bible to discuss what could be termed scientific issues. Our intellectual culture is not accustomed to use passages from the Bible, in this case, the book of Genesis, as places from which to begin a discussion of the world around and within ourselves.[4] We have other constructs, but many of these have features in common with those of the Middle Ages, as we will see. Thirdly, Augustine is exemplifying by his choice of example—the phrase, "increase and multiply"—the very process he is endeavoring to explain. His example is to be found in an almost rhapsodic summary of essential issues at the close of his work the *Confessions.* "Increase and multiply" can be interpreted in diverse and various ways by diverse and various figures of speech. These are *figurae*, or gestures within *modus* or manner of moving (*figurae in modis*). One can, depending upon the mode or manner, interpret this short phrase historically, depending upon the context of the book of Genesis as the beginning of creation and the history of the world. One can, as Augustine proceeds to do, interpret the phrase allegorically, referring to a multiplicity of things and thoughts within one's mind—the rich fertility possible within the human spirit. The tropological interpretation would be to take action, seize the day, so to speak, taken with the Latin command mode. Finally, its future, related to the eschatological mode, Augustine goes on to explain, lay in the nourishment of joy.

Augustine has come into the discussion several times, not only in this chapter, but in other contexts as well. We have also remarked upon the fact that while one might disagree with him, one could not afford to ignore what Augustine had to say on nearly every topic of importance. In his clear, intense style, Augustine made many points that had important reverberation throughout the entire medieval period and that had to be reconciled with new tools for investigation, discovery, and demonstration that would be released to an interested reading public with the translation of Aristotle's works from Greek into Latin in the late 12th and early 13th centuries. His importance for both medieval and so-called early modern thought, as evident well into the 17th century, cannot be overemphasized. Writers absorbed his priorities, treating them as givens, appropriated his terminology, and incorporated large chunks of his major works into their own writing (as he had also done with biblical scriptures and other writings). Sometimes they quoted him. It is safe to say that, in addition to the biblical scriptures, no other writer had as consistent influence and authority during the entire medieval period as Augustine, and with influence that sometimes appears to be by remote control.

Having established Augustine's influence on the medieval period, which of his views flowed into medieval mental culture? There were many, but one of the most important is that sound is substantial; it is separate from the indicator of that sound. Music is an example of this. This view gave authority to the ministry discipline of music as one of the material and measurement arts—a discipline that made available even to children examples of particularity, conjunctive lines, and motion. Sound, for Augustine, is material. Although sound is unseen, it is substantial. It can, therefore, be measured. Sound, furthermore, is the stuff from which songs are made, although, admittedly, this stuff passes away with the singing. Essential also to Augustine's thinking is his observation that an equivalence exists between sound and time, since both are substances. Finally, all of this, as well as music's place within the discussion, leads directly to an understanding of the physical universe and of generation and its effects. Music makes, as Augustine states, an understanding of the physical universe possible. A musical example, since everyone can envision it, and because music makes the unseen apprehensible to the senses, is not optional but necessary.

In his treatise concerning music, Augustine follows this line of reasoning, leading to the conclusions that were to have such continued resonance throughout the Middle Ages. Changes in the designation of musical substance by means of the *figurae* of music notation can be traced to decisive, cogent statements made by Augustine that give those changes a rational basis.[5] We will consider some of the statements throughout *De musica* that gave such definition to the place and importance of music. First, in book I, chapter I, he writes, *"Sonorum certar dimensiones observare non ad grammaticam spectat, sed ad musicam."* (A writer coming from the standpoint that both grammar and music use the material of sound can observe that dimensions [and properties] of sound are more clearly to be viewed in music than in grammar.) In another context Augustine notes that music makes these dimensions plain, that is, the autonomy of separate and discrete units of sound, since sound in music changes (i.e., uses different tones). Because of the use of different tones, both the containment of individual tones and their directionality are made obvious in music, although speech (i.e., grammar) also uses separate, differing sounds, such as consonants and vowels. What dimensions of grammar do not pertain to music? Actually, none; but it is the "innumerable genres of sound, in which certain dimensions can be observed, which are not available within grammar, but can be perceived easily in music." How can these "numerous dimensions" be constructed (*artificiosum,* or "artifacted")? These are "voices," and they have names. There is the implication that it is due at least in part to this matter of naming and containing (within separate tone, or voice) that music receives its identity and upon which its usefulness depends. Further, the substance of time, as well as sound, can be observed more acutely in music than in grammar, as *tempora* or time units can be defined by a stroke (*pulsus*), or by the plucking of a string.

Just this issue of the identity of music is Augustine's consideration within the next chapter of *De musica*, book I, chapter II, in which he asks the question that resonated through centuries of writing concerning music as an analogical discipline: *"Musica quid sit, modulari quid sit."* (What is music, and what constitutes the bringing together of music tones in an appropriate and convenient manner?)[6] Music is a discipline that possesses both force and reason—contradictory attributes that can be made to become reconciled, implied in the concept/term *modulatio.* *"Musica est scientia bene modulandi . . . si mihi liqueret quid sit ipsa modulatio."* (Music is the science of aptly bringing together opposing, discrete, entities in such a way that one experiences, as well as registering with the intellect, that this process indeed has taken place.) There is no completely satisfactory equivalent expression for *modulatio,* but one is able to hear it. How can one otherwise understand the term except in singing, and in dancing, that is, *modulatio* according to ways of experiencing and moving (i.e., *modus*): *"sed quid video modulari a modo esse dictum, cum in omnibus bene factis modus servandus sit, et multa etiam in canendo ac saltando quamvis delectent."* (We notice what it is that makes music effective because whatever makes it so is delicious—absolutely delectable.)[7] Augustine continues (in chapter III), *"Bene modulari quid sit, et cur in musicae definitione positum cur ergo additum est, bene; cum jam ipsa modulatio nisi bene moveatur."* (Music, then consists in integer portions of sound, brought by design together in modulated appropriateness, which both necessitates and presents movement. To the extent that this is made reasonable, music is a discipline.)[8] But music also is able to "relax and repair the mind by its enhanced moderating power and by its voluptuousness" (*"relaxandi ac reparandi animi gratia moderatissime ab iis aliquid voluptatis"*). *Cantus* exemplifies "suaveness": the achievement of moving from one tone to the other well, which is the cohesion of *sound* with *time.*

But what, in all of this, is actually visible, Augustine asks. Instruments, such as those that produce sound by pipes and strings and for which external material is available to the eyes, are considered to sing—to have a voice. These instruments are also *figurae*—shapes that delineate the sound that can be produced in imitation of the human voice. It can be seen, then, that imitation is useful for teaching and learning; masters at imitation are said to teach well. Furthermore, however, for a body of knowledge (art) to be useful, it must have a system of internal laws, namely, a rationale.[9] Can one say that "science" is rooted in rationality and that "art," on the other hand, in imitation? But there are many arts that partake of both—a rationale underlying the art, and teaching of the art based upon imitation, and the two are constantly, simultaneously, exercised. Music is a discipline based on a rational structure of rules but must be taught by imitation. As such, the body, whether singing or playing instruments, is united with the intellect. But we need to be careful about strictly separating the two, the body and the mind, since imitation is not relegated solely to the body but is also impossible without the body. In other words, there is a simultaneity of function, a mutual reciprocity in which both are necessary to "science," a reciprocity that absorbs a mind–body separation.

For Augustine, music, which he defines at the onset of his discussion, best illustrates a disciplinary rule-based, essentially step-by-step, precept-by-precept system of knowledge, combined with the experience and practice of that knowledge. It is not enough to know the basic rules of music, the existence of particular tones, the relationship of tones to one another made clear by movement; one needs also to practice music, taking instruction in imitation of those who are masters. Furthermore, the pursuit of the mastery of the discipline of music necessarily brings out a discussion of where sense, memory, intelligence, and judgment ultimately reside, for whatever is "delightful to the senses" commends itself to the memory, as well as to bodily movement. This practice, alone, however, is not a science, but rather, a basis in precept is also needed.[10] There is, accordingly, an important difference between acting (theatrics) and music, since music is a science, whereas "theatrics" exhibit.[11]

Teaching is important to Augustine. Music as a science is not an arcane jumble of practices devised for the purpose of separating initiates from others, "those in the know" from an audience who might be captivated by what they see and hear but have no idea at all what the "exhibit" signifies. Teaching (and an organized curriculum) mattered enough to this writer that he wrote a treatise on the topic, *The Order that Exists Among the Disciplines* (*De ordine*), with an explanation of what a discipline consisted, why order was necessary, as well as music's place within this organization. Order is understandably apparent in Augustine's treatise on music, in that he begins with the question of what music is, "*Quid est musica*"; proceeds to discuss voice, as *particular* division and limitation of sound, *relationship* in terms of *modulatio*, and then *movement* in terms of the movement of time (*tempus*). There are two types of movement that are, as Augustine states, "completely manifest," namely, long and stretches of time. He goes on to discuss what *parts* of time (time as *materia/substantia*) consist of, how these spaces or parts are not indefinite or indeterminate, and how this movement within the material of time is by no means "irrational."[12] Augustine then proceeds (in chapter XIII) to discuss motion in terms of proportion, as well as time related to motion drawn across, or "conducted," through one's field of view, also writing of "modes of time" (*modi temporum*).[13] "*Tempus est autem ad illos motus redire tractandos.*" (Time is motion that is being [constantly] drawn out before us.) We perceive time in terms of "spaces or intervals of motion."

These are pivotal concepts. The first concept is of the difference between substance and delineatory *figura,* exemplified eventually in music notation; the second concept is of music as using the invisible substance of time, which, therefore, makes it capable of exemplifying divisions or parts of time, as well as exemplifying length of duration, also exemplified eventually in the 13th century in music notation, as well as music that exemplified the properties of motion—how it could be measured, quantified, and delimited within the contained "body" of the pulse. All of these considerations set up music as the discipline that eventually discerned and made available the substance of the soul and of the triune God (treated in book VI of *De musica*). It is not happenstance that Augustine wrote his two treatises on the attributes of "soulish substance" together with his treatises on the disciplines. Important among them is music as the exemplary, dispositive discipline that made difficult things comprehensible.

One can observe, in reading *De musica,* that it lacks specific music examples. It was the challenge and responsibility of those writing within the material and measurement science of music for the next one-and-one-half millennia to accomplish this, and, in fact, this is exactly what *musica disciplina* brought about—examples to each and every principle Augustine set forth. Concepts such as the *pes, figura, figura in modis, instrumentum* as *figura,* interval/*spacia,* time proceeding by increment as number, time as measured by divisions, time substance contained within pulse and delineated by *figura,* modes of time/movement, and relationships *unam ad unum,* and many more, were all eventually exemplified by—one could even say translated into—music. Augustine's topics constitute models as they appear one after the other for the continuity, organization, and rational basis for writing concerning music as the exemplary discipline. Why was music so effective? At the conclusion of book I, Augustine states that music penetrates to the most secret recesses of our inner life. Music engages our power of reason while it caresses our senses. Music enhances our capacity to judge, hence become truly wise, enabling us to understand what is neither immediately apparent nor visible to the physical eye, since music uses as its material sound, time, and movement—all invisible commodities.

Furthermore, Augustine's writing on the important subject of material and motion also brought those medieval writers who gave musical examples to the principles Augustine had delineated into contact with an ongoing discussion concerning infinitude and division of motion. This background put a thought-context in place and prepared readers for understanding Aristotle's *Physics* when it became more widely available in Latin translation during the first generation of the 13th century, particularly at the emerging universities. One could say, in addition, that Augustine's *De musica* also gave a Latin readership an appetite for Aristotle's *Physics.*

Appetite for Aristotle they certainly had; from its multiple translations from Greek into Latin in the late 12th and early 13th centuries, the *Physics* received more continuous commentary than any other work of "the Philosopher." It would seem that those who read Latin certainly read this, at least to get its most important arguments. What is Aristotle's *Physics* about, and why was it so important at the onset of the 13th century, an importance that scarcely diminished throughout the next two centuries? This is not a question for the faint-hearted, since the *Physics* treats some of the most basic and far-reaching questions of material reality. First of all, the *Physics* was, and is, of great importance because it, like Plato's *Timaeus,* is about material and how to recognize and deal with it. Further, the *Physics,* rather than contesting

a philosophical tradition or presenting a totally unfamiliar, unpre-
pared, doctrine, brings together an entire corpus of writing, similar
to the Latin translation of Plato's *Timaeus* and its influence. The background material for the *Physics* raises, as does the *Timaeus*, or for that
matter, the Old Testament book of Genesis, fundamental questions of
undifferentiated, or chaotic, limitless *natura*, substance, movement,
the nature of movement, time—again as material—and place, as well
as the propensity for aggregation or density within place. Many of the
most important themes of the *Physics* are presented in the first three
books. Arguments are prepared in the first two books; brought then
to conclusions in the third. Here, taken from the beginning of book III,
in English translation, are some the most relevant passages dealing
with nature, mass, part, relationship, and motion, treating these far-
reaching topics in the order of their appearance in the *Physics*:

> Nature is a principle of motion and change, and it is the subject of our
> inquiry. We must therefore see that we understand what motion is; for if
> it were unknown nature too would be unknown. When we have deter-
> mined the nature of motion, our task will be to attack in the same way
> the terms which come next in order. Now motion is supposed to belong
> to the class of things which are continuous; and the infinite presents it-
> self first in the continuous—that is how it comes about that the account
> of the infinite is often used in definitions of the continuous; for what is
> infinitely divisible is continuous. Besides these, place, void, and time
> are thought to be necessary conditions of motion. Clearly then, for these
> reasons and also because the attributes mentioned are common to every-
> thing and universal, we must first take each of them in hand and discuss
> it. For the investigation of special attributes comes after that of the com-
> mon attributes. (200b24ff)
>
> Next: the appropriateness to the science or discipline of and for this
> problem is clearly indicated; for all who have touched on this kind of
> science in a way worth considering have formulated views about the in-
> finite, and indeed, to a man, make it a principle of things. (203a.l)
>
> Nevertheless . . . the common body is a principle of all things, differ-
> ing from part to part in size and shape. (203b.3)
>
> But the problem of the infinite is difficult: many contradictions result
> whether we suppose it to exist or not to exist. If it exists, we have still
> to ask how it exists—as a substance or as the essential attribute of some
> entity? Or in neither way, yet none the less is there something which is
> infinite or some things which are infinitely many? (203b31ff)
>
> Our account does not rob the mathematicians of their science, by dis-
> proving the actual existence of the infinite in the direction of increase,
> in the sense of the untraversable. In point of fact they do not need the
> infinite and do not use it. They postulate only that a finite straight line
> may be produced as far as they wish. It is possible to have divided into
> the same ratio as the largest quantity another magnitude of any size you

like. Hence, for the purposes of proof, it will make no difference to them whether the infinite is found among existent magnitudes. (207b.28ff.)

Now like existence of motion is asserted by all who have anything to say about nature, because they all concern themselves with the construction of the world and study the question of becoming and perishing, which processes could not come about without the existence of motion. But those who say that there is an infinite number of worlds, some of which are in process of becoming while others are in the process of perishing, assert that there is always motion (for these processes of becoming and perishing of the worlds necessarily involve motion), whereas those who hold that there is only one world, whether everlasting or not, make corresponding assumptions in regard to motion . . . Mind introduced motion and separated them. (250b.l7ff)

We must consider then, how this matter stands; for the discovery of the truth about it is of importance, not only for the study of nature . . . Each kind of motion, therefore, necessarily involves the presence of the things that are capable of that motion. (251.a.6)[14]

So then, material contains qualities, especially of motion, of the ability to aggregate, the capacity for breaking out and fragmentation, and of opacity. Especially important is the observation that material also contains motion. Further, the subject of material, aggregation, mass, and opacity as a potential and capacity could be expressed within both outward and inward property. This was by no means lost on readers, such as Philip the Chancellor, whose position was that of intermediary between the episcopal see of Notre Dame, under construction at that time, and the newly constituted theology faculty of the emerging University of Paris.[15] The commentaries on the Physics followed. First, perhaps, is the commentary of Robert Grosseteste in the 1230s; then came Roger Bacon's commentary in the last third of the 13th century; and the commentaries on the *Physics* continue at least until the end of the 16th century, with renewed interest in understanding the *Physics* and its discussion of material and motion in the late 18th and 19th centuries. Perhaps it is we who have lost touch with "the Philosopher," as Aristotle was known.

Throughout the Middle Ages, Augustine's *De musica,* largely ignored today, together with the Latin translation of the *Timaeus* of Plato offered a storehouse of vocabulary, conceptualization, and subject matter, as well as a reasoned, systematic basis for the study of music in the Middle Ages. This continued well into what is known as the early modern period. Augustine's writings prepared a context for, and were combined with, the increased availability of the Latin translation of Aristotle's works during the final generation of the 12th and early 13th centuries. Augustine and Aristotle, taken together, offered new conceptual tools for understanding the physical as well as the mental worlds that surround daily human life. Music made life better, certainly, but it also made these tools comprehensible. Writers throughout the Middle Ages took up this vocabulary, expressed these concepts, and produced music examples.

It is paradoxical that just as the study of the history of music as a discipline was being formulated, in the beginning of the 20th century, the "books" that had given the discipline of music its rational basis received less and less attention. (Compare, for example, the number of entries in a major library database catalogue for other theological works of Augustine with those related to music.) In lieu of the conceptual structure upon which the study of music was based, writings offering exemplification of these terms and concepts are often given a 20th-century background, such as a falsifying narrative-chronological construct, dependent upon the notion of "schools"; an "organic evolutionary" growth and development model; or a model using composers and works as organizing principle—rather incongruous within an anonymous compositional culture. In order to understand medieval music, the basis of Western music, a medieval background must be joined with the disciplinary writings that offer exemplification of that background.

NOTES

1. Many of the models mentioned here are not by any means restricted in their use to the Middle Ages. Saints' lives as narrative constructs continued to be composed after this period, until, in fact, the present day, often in connection with a process of canonization. The reader is invited to consider more contemporary applications of these compositional categories, of which there are many.

2. Some of the immense resonance but also complexity of these interpretational modi, alternating as they do in the Bible, can be observed in the two-volume study of Henri de Lubac, *Exégèse médiévale: Les quatre sens de l'écriture* (Paris, 1959), in which de Lubac investigates as an introduction to the concept of interpretational "sense" or mode allegory within the New Testament letters of the Apostle Paul, with further topics such as myth and allegory, "mystère," pedagogy, and spirituality, as well as the formation of doctrine, the literal mode, or foundation of the "letter" for the historical, literal mode, particularities of language, a concept of history, with particular attention paid to the "order" of history (*ordo*), "*mysterium requiramus*" ("we need/we question mystery"), or the allegorical mode, as well as the "mystery" of the future. These alternating modes are also discussed within Beryl Smalley's *The Study of the Bible in the Middle Ages*. It can be concluded that most people in the Middle Ages who had any reflective life at all, whether literate or not, also were aware of the significance and indicative power of these four interpretational

modi. We today are also aware of these modes of interpretation and use them as we speak and read.

3. Augustine's *Confessions.* See closing chapters of this work for a more complete context. Augustine had much more to say about the use of interpretational *modi* built on the *figurae* of the historical mode in his commentaries on the book of Genesis, or *De genesi ad litteram*, PL XXXIV, CSEL XXVIII, ed. Josephus Zycha (Vienna/Prague, 1894), and certainly, in his commentaries or sermons on the Psalms.

4. Another medieval construct is that of etymology in which a word is expounded, not in terms of its chronological development and transformation, but rather in terms of all of the ways or manners in which that word could be used, a cumulative process in which, at the end of the discussion, one is made aware of the variety of meanings possible for a given expression, with each expression contributing to an overall comprehension of the word. Isidore of Seville's *Etymologiae,* mentioned previously as an exponent of this methodology, is another important influence upon medieval intellectual culture, as the work was frequently and authoritatively quoted throughout the Middle Ages.

5. It should be kept in mind that Augustine's treatise on music was written in conjunction with two treatises on the soul, that is, on unseen substance, as well as a treatise on the subject of the order that exists amongst the disciplines. All were written more or less together around the time of Augustine's conversion, that is ca. 387. His mental environment at that time was centered upon this invisible, but substantial, world of the mind, in which music played such a definitive role because it brought components of this world to sensory experience, uniting sense, experience, and intellection.

6. *Modulari,* used here, became an important and multivalent concept, accruing connotations through the Middle Ages.

7. Only what is delectable can be learned well, writes Augustine in *The Order that Exists within the Disciplines (De ordine).* This pronouncement not only could be borne out by observation, but it was quoted often throughout the Middle Ages, for example, by Hugh of St. Victor, in his *Didiscalicon,* in which he states that the *materia* to be learned must be sweet to the taste.

8. These topics—that is, individual tones, relationship between these tones, and the movement that results necessarily when tones are joined, achieved, when successful with *suavitas*—would occupy Augustine for several more chapters, as for example, in chapter 4.

9. Augustine, *De musica,* Book I, Chapter IV, 6: "*Sed quid tibi videtur?*" "But what is seen?"

10. The distinction that is made here—namely, between the one who delights in an activity and learns it well, by imitation and repetition; and the one who understands what is to be accomplished and, in fact, can teach it as a system of origins and underlying precepts—is an important point in the opening discussion of Aristotle's *Metaphysics.* It was taken up by Boethius in his influential treatise on music, *De institutione musica,* Book I, XXXIV, and others, such as al-Farabi, as the distinction between *cantor* and *musicus*: the *cantor* is able to accomplish repetitive tasks well (i.e., sing), whereas the *musicus* truly understands the underlying principles of music.

11. Both, however, use the same materials: sound, time, and movement; and therefore, manners of construction are part of a common discussion, hence, the importance of Aristotle's *Poetics* for music conceptualization in terms of incremental divisions or intervals of duration when the Latin translation of the *Poetics* became available in the 13th century, and even more so at the end of the 16th century, beginning of the 17th century, with a conceptualization of *basso continuo*. Each introduction of a seminal Latin text of Aristotle brought an exemplification of the most significant feature of that text within the illustrative discipline of music.

12. Chapter IX, "*motus rationabilis et irrationabilis connumerati et dinumerati*": "rational and irrational motion, addition with respect to motion, and diminution." Aristotle, in the *Physics,* speaks of tremor as nonproductive motion (irrational), since it lacks directionality that can be measured even into infinitude. Augustine's parts of time, divisions of time movement, and the rationality or directionality of this movement, in combination with the translation and availability of Aristotle's *Physics* during the first generation of the 13th century, were all exemplified most cogently and comprehensibly by music. One reason, however, why it would seem that Augustine's *De musica* was not frequently quoted, despite the large number of manuscripts showing its transmission, is a feature held in common with the *Timaeus,* as well *Phaedo,* of Plato, namely, the dialogue between question and answer. As a question is inserted, an explanatory continuity is interrupted, making quotation difficult. One must either quote a considerable amount of the text or leap over the question, causing a rupture in the argument. But Augustine's *De musica* was also simply taken for granted, so ubiquitous are the traces it left behind in writing concerning music.

13. Chapter XIII, 22:

Tempus est autem ad illos motus redire tractandos et discutiendos qui huic disciplinae proprie tribuuntur, et propter quos ista de numeris, de alia scilicet disciplina, quantum per negotio satis visum est, consideravimus . . . in horarum spatio motus . . . vel aliquis hujusce modi temporum notatione sentire illos duos motus, quod unus simplus, alius duplus sit: vel etiamsi id non possis dicere, illa tamen congruentia delectari, atque origina voluptate affici ut unus sonitus simplum altis duplum temporis teneat, quos iambis pedes vocant eosque continuet atque cantexat . . .

A "space" of motion, ways or modi of observing, even notating, time, could be coordinated conceptually with Aristotle's modes of directional motions in his discussion of the nature of motion within the *Physics,* as the *Physics* became available in Latin translation during the late 12th century and early 13th century. This juxtaposition of "modes of time and motion" was exemplified as "rhythmic modes" in writing concerning music as the illustrative discipline in the mid- to late-13th century within the early university.

14. For the Greek text, cf. edition W. D. Ross (Oxford, 1950, repr. 1966); English translation, R. P. Hardie and R. K. Gaye, in *The Complete Works of Aristotle, Revised Oxford Translation,* ed. Jonathan Barnes, Bollingen Series 71.2, 2 vols. (Princeton, 1984), vol. I, pp. 315ff, Latin text in appendix.

15. As an example of the influence of the *Physics,* cf. *Philippi Cancellarii Summa de bono ad fidem codicum primum edita studio et cura Nicolai Wicki,* Opera philosophica mediae aetatis selecta, volumen II-Pars Prior/Posterior (Bern, 1985); one might easily miss the importance of the *Physics* within this work, since it is not what would become a typical commentary on the *Physics,* with quotations from that work followed by comments. Rather, Philip brings up a topic important for its theological implication and exemplification and proceeds then to formulate his comments using vocabulary, as well as argumentation that he had culled from his careful, thoughtful, reading of the *Physics.* Philip is also known for composing *conductus,* a genre of songs that provide examples for Aristotle's concept of *theoria* (*ductus*).

7

Musica disciplina: Analogies and Explanations

Why is medieval music worth studying? For one, the structural principles of music in the Middle Ages are the basis of Western music, a basis that has parallels in other world music cultures. Medieval music is situated within cultural priorities that were taught when one is very young. These deeply held cultural priorities can be found by identifying what cultures bring together and what they separate, particularly in terms of learning experiences.[1] So, perhaps it is not so remarkable that educational disciplines that have been increasingly separated in the 20th and 21st centuries are in fact connected in the Middle Ages. Conversely, disciplines that were carefully and consciously connected for reasons that were at that time clear and plain, are separated today. Not only are the boundaries between the sacred and secular amorphous,[2] but the boundaries between intellectual and nonintellectual are as well.[3] Literacy, of course, is one decisive factor, but the ability on some level to read and write does not impinge upon either of the two separations, sacred and secular, intellectual and nonintellectual. Even—or especially—the separation between high and low culture is a recent separation.

Disciplines today have, increasingly, become more and more specialized, with ways of investigation, jargon, as well as declared priorities, that all rarely transcend modern disciplinary boundaries. One is faced with becoming increasingly incomprehensible to one's colleagues in other fields, and this despite the prevailing trend of developing interdisciplinary studies.

Overspecialization was not an issue in the Middle Ages. There existed then a far more unified educational system, established centuries previously, with component parts logically related to an entire system that was perceived as both complete and directed. Medieval education had a goal. In this regard, questions that comes to mind might include: How much education was involved in an "education"? What had one learned if one had an "education"? What can we expect medieval people to know, and what, then, were their priorities? A culture trains capabilities useful to that culture. What capabilities did medieval education in the widest sense prize? What place did music have within this educational system, and why is this place difficult to understand today?

We have seen that, in spite of some variations in what would be known today as textbooks,[4] a Latin readership, possessing some literacy as the result of at least a primary-school education, had had some acquaintanceship with a handful of basic principles. These means for gaining understanding, and for encouraging critical thinking, have been identified in order to approach the question of how educational areas were related to each other, and how music might serve a useful function within this educational context. The background that has been collected is one that reached back to Roman education and was given Christian purpose in terms of addressing the problem of invisible "substance" by Augustine. The same relatively small group of writings was expanded in terms of intellectual tools (*organa*) as more and more texts of Plato, and eventually Aristotle, became accessible, read in the Latin language, and discussed in terms of commentary as well as lectures within the classrooms of the early 13th-century university. This structure, in each of its component parts, was made comprehensible by means of music examples. Writings concerning music, rather than autonomous in their content, as textbooks tend to be today, were essentially anthologies of examples, with explanation, for understanding a conceptual background that was assumed to be familiar because it was obvious and held in common.

That an educational background that had been in place for the most part for hundreds of years was assumed is a factor that is also responsible for the difficulty in determining how these writings on music functioned within curricula; for what purpose they were in fact written. Further, the analogical purpose of music as a discipline also generated the interpretation of what was written, since a background in any case, then and now, was required of the reader—a background that was not immediately available to a reader of the 20th century. In addition, comprehension has not been facilitated by 20th-century translations into English, in which Latin terms have been rendered into more familiar English terms, therefore depriving them of the clusters of significance that had accumulated through many centuries—significances that would have been instantly available to the Latin readership to whom the work was addressed. One example of this is the rendering of the Latin term *figura* into words that were apparently regarded as English equivalent expressions: "sign," "form," "symbol," "representation," or "idea." These expressions are by no means synonymous in the Middle Ages, particularly since all express and/or translate different Greek original terms (such as *schema*, translated into *figura*).

Nothing could be truly understood without the exemplification of music, wrote Augustine. The writers of the Middle Ages took this seriously. Some of whom have left few biographical traces in terms of their places of birth; their occupations; of what discipline they were professors within the early university; where, exactly, they carried out these professorships; or even how long they lived. Their writings, following the organizational procedure of Augustine's *De musica* to a remarkable extent, gave exemplary power to the principles held in common and built on a shared intellectual past. The most striking of these components have been collected as we have placed them one by one within a system that corresponds to that of the Middle Ages, beginning first with the concept of *materia*, proceeding then to individuation within that *materia*, indicated by the concept of *figura*, showing connection by means of individual, as well as varied and diverse, *figurae* within continuity, resulting finally in a conceptualization of motion, *modus*, both as directionality, as well as susceptible to incremental measurement within a trajectory motion. That different motions could be present simultaneously, proceeding from different even opposing points of origin, and moving in exactly opposing directions, to arrive then finally at an endpoint of reconciliation and consonance, was also expressed by the concept of "contrary motion," within Aristotle's *Physics*. Points, or *puncta*, indicated by *figurae*, of convenience or concordance, *in via* or *in modis*, both within these contrary motions and at a final closure, could be presented by the term *punctum contra punctum*. Literally, this expression presented one point in contiguity, both vertically as well as horizontally against another "point," a term that eventually became familiar as "counterpoint." But one also actually "did" counterpoint, experiencing writing counterpoint as training, science, and art. In a verbal explanation, all of this appears complicated; in musical examples such ideas became clear and plain. Even the principles involved, particularity, connection, and movement, as well as their expression as communication or as measured *materia*, became plain in musical examples.

This is the scope of writing concerning music, *musica disciplina*, in which the discipline of music as a "ministry discipline" ministers to the other disciplines dealing with particular things, relationships, and motion within material, to make both general principle as well as individual occurrence plain. Musical examples skimmed off the salient factor from an entire discussion that could become quite complicated—such as the *Timaeus* of Plato, *The Marriage of Philology and Mercury* of Martianus Capella, on to the *Physics* and *Metaphysics*, or the *Treatise on the Soul* (*De anima*) of Aristotle. Music selected the most conspicuous hypothetical construct—one which the author also identified as such—and made it plain.[5] Furthermore, the musical example was comprehensible because it was, as Augustine stated, both attractive, in fact delicious to the senses, and could be verified within experience. One *sang* these examples of the principles of the world within which one's life took place, often day in and day out.

A selective panorama of concepts with writers who dealt with these concepts include:

1. Martianus Capella used concepts of spatial relationships, interval, the relationship of "high" and "low" as vertical spatial relationships in terms of trees giving forth music tones. This vertical relationship of height corresponding to "high" tones indicated by *figurae* on a manuscript page can be seen first in the western part of Europe, in some of the earliest manuscripts from what is today France.[6]
2. Cassiodorus, in his Psalm Commentaries, uses *schemata*, as *figurae* in their multiplicity, giving access and individuation (*distinctiones, differentiae*) to unseen substance; *instrumentum* is also a *schema*.
3. Music writers of the late 9th and 10th centuries writing in what they consider to be the discipline of music, begin with sound substance, proceed then to individual *tonus/vox* accessed by individual *figura* (*neuma, littera*, and others), resulting in the concept of relationship based on these *figurae* that indicate and express apt contiguity (*modulatio*) as well as immediately perceptible differences (*differentiae, distinctiones*) in ways of moving (*modi*). *Musica disciplina* therefore provides direct, perceptible analogies for understanding particularity, shared by both grammar and arithmetic, and relationship, held in common by logic and geometry; and also presents comprehensible constructs for understanding both the nature of motion as well as differences between motions. Motion, as Aristotle pointed out, is an essential attribute of *materia/substantia*. Motion is realized in terms of the unseen motion within the sound-material of speech, which can be compared to the visible motions within the studies of astronomy and physics. All of these, namely, the studies of particularity, relationship, and movement as exhibited within the invisible *materia* of sound, time, motion, were available within the discipline of music. Music as a discipline also prepared the way mentally for the study of, and work with, the unseen substances of cognition, memory, and, finally, the nature of God. These writers on the topic of music exemplification, with some of their priorities, from the late 9th century to the early 12th century, include:[7]

1. Aurelianus of Réomé (early and mid-ninth century) developed the concept of sound substance in terms of dealing with it, as well as "making things" with it (*facientes*); individuation in terms of *figura, littera, numerus, syllabae, pars,* resulting in relationship (*modulatio*), within *modus, figurae in modis* (which effect *modulatio*)—all of which can be perceived instantaneously within cognition.

2. Regino of Prüm (d. ca. 915) developed the concept of *modus,* ways of moving (*manneriae*), *figurae in modis,* differences (*differentiae*) between *modi* in placing *cantus* in categories according to their differences.

3. Hucbald of St. Armand (late 9th and early 10th centuries) used notions *disciplina, notas musicas, per litteras voces* (individual tones indicated by *figurae*) proceeding to relationship (*melodiae in ordo*) resulting in *distinctiones* in movement, which he states, one can apprehend by the senses, even without instruction.

4. Guido of Arezzo (fl. ca. 991–1033) discussed inner/outer *figurae, litterae, syllabae, partes, pedes, phtongi,* all referring to differentiation and individuation within the generality of sound substance, as "particular constituent parts of a melodic continuity"; *figurae* make differences clear, that is, *differentiae* in relationship and manners of movement based on *figurae* (these differences can be ascertained at a glance as ways of moving, *modi, tropi*).[8] Guido dealt with issues of distinction (*distinctiones*) and congruency (*consonantiae*), of particularity and coherence, and of diversity.

5. Johannes Affligimensis (writing ca. 1100) developed the relationship of *cantus* (*substantia*) to particularity, to relationship itself, to differences of motion.

Guido of Arezzo, in his *Micrologus,* in the sheer volume of his treatise, as well as its all-encompassing intention, given by its title; but also in using particularly apt analogies, summarized this shared intellectual heritage, and in turn was quoted at least into the late 16th century (by Zarlino, for example). His examples not only are clear, but they are related to life experience. We see this in his discussion of modes, the perception of which is dependent upon both the clarity and recognition of *figurae.* Individual *figurae,* as dispositive, individual, delineatory, and indicative, can be seen at a glance and recognized, and conclusions can be reached:

> An example of the ways in which properties and individualities of the modes, as I have indicated, can be perceived and heard, is made by the fact that people can be recognized by their ways of moving. One can say, this one is a Greek, that one a Spaniard, this one a Latin, that one a German, and this one, indeed, as point of fact, from Gaul. And the

diversities of these various modes can be adapted to states of the mind so that a single mode such as the second authentic mode, attracts broken leaping *figurae*, or the plagal of the third mode prefers voluptuousness. Garrulousness is proper to the fourth authentic mode, and its plagal demonstrates pleasantness, and so on for the other modes.[9]

As with all of the authors cited here, Guido used a common conceptual background, with an established vocabulary that was also shared by all of the *artes/scientiae* within an educational system. By the time of his writing, this background was self-evident. Accordingly, his treatise must be read through the lens of this intellectual heritage, not that of the 20th century,[10] which, typically relates Guido to "performance"— an obviously 20th-century priority. Guido is relating music, especially by means of *figurae*, to all of the other disciplines within an educational system; one made use of music examples by actually doing them— participating in these examples through personal experience.

That the *Physics* of Aristotle was translated at least four times within a relatively short period of time in the late 12th and early 13th centuries, at least three times from the Greek, once from Greek into Arabic, then into Latin, gives evidence for the enormous influence of this work by one who was subsequently simply identified as "the Philosopher."[11] No other appellation was necessary since commentaries on this writer continued to be written for many centuries, filling the libraries of Europe today. In fact, the Latin commentary literature on Aristotle has only been partially identified, even today.[12] No wonder that new concepts, new vocabulary, as well as old terms filled with new meanings, were then given exemplification within the discipline of music. It is remarkable how swiftly this took place; apparently it was essential that music illustrate these important new concepts in order for them to become comprehensible to a Latin-reading public, particularly from the newly organized University of Paris during the first generation of the 13th century. What was of interest? What did these writers on music make of it? How were these principles that were so worthy of such discussion, dissension, and argumentation translated into music examples, as well as music explanations?

We begin, as we have in the preceding chapters, with *materia/substantia/natura*, or preexistent substance, which, as Aristotle states, is the "subject of our inquiry." Motion belongs to *materia*, is inherent within *materia*; motion presents itself first in "the class of things that are continuous," leading eventually to "infinitude." According to Aristotle, what is infinitely divisible is continuous. The possibility of continuous motion, inherent within material substance, can be divided, as *divisiones*, even into infinitude, and can be measured. This applies, as well to the invisible *materia* of time, combined with sound. We see, therefore, in writings concerning music from the middle years of the 13th century on, a vital, dynamic relationship between Augustine's lengthy discussion of duration as long and short, as well as the contained "body" of the pulse, full of movement, and the concept of incremental measurement of time and sound. These concepts are not only viewed as possibilities but are necessary to understanding continuity itself. From the mid-13th century though the next two centuries, writers concerning music, identified by Palémon Glorieux as "Masters of the University of Paris," relate these stunning and new, at that time, ways of viewing the physical realities of the world to music. They include such writers as Johannes de Garlandia, an anonymous writer designated as "Anonymous IV," the so-called Franco of Cologne, "Lambertus," Jerome of Moravia, Johannes de Grocheio (from beginning of 14th century), Marchetus of Padua (ca. 1317–1318), Jacobus of Liège (early to mid-14th century), and Johannes de Muris (early to mid-14th century). These are "initiates," well-acquainted with new mental tools that had become available, not only to those who read Latin, but increasingly to a general public. Concepts such as Aristotle's "theory" (*theoria*) model, beginning with a decisive beginning, proceeding step by measured step to a conclusion, eventually infused what could be designated as a "thought climate," to become an unquestioned component of the "scientific process" of experimentation today. All of these writers, indeed anyone who had attended upper-level classes at the universities that were started up all over Europe in the late 13th and 14th centuries, shared a common vocabulary, as well as priorities held in common, some of which came immediately to the fore at the very onset of their treatises.

Johannes de Garlandia, for example, began his treatise with a loaded expression, *Habito*, obviously bringing to mind *habitus*, as way of being,[13] also then bringing up *plana musica* (unmeasured), in contrast with music that is measured in terms of increments, or measured music (*mensurabilis*). This, for a 13th-century readership, would have brought up the question of laws that were "timed," as well as those who were "untimed," as Augustine had stated, "*Duplex est lex: temporalis videlicet et eternal.*"[14] This topic of the interaction of the temporary with the eternal, given new impetus from the translation of Aristotle's *Physics*, contained a concept of the incremental measurement of trajectory motions. (For example, if one threw a ball in a certain direction, it should be possible to measure each portion of that arc. Likewise, a melody proceeding in a certain direction could be measured [i.e., by individual tones and the length of each tone's duration].) The considerations addressed by Johannes de Garlandia, as well as others, brought into discussion an important pair of authors and topics, namely, Augustine

with Aristotle, on questions of particular increment and how to desig-
nate it,[15] measurement within continuity, or its absence as *planus*,[16] and
structure within movement describing and designating movement itself.[17] Garlandia goes on to discuss a tool, *organum* or *instrumentum*, for
measured music, giving, as he states, order or organization to sound
substance. Again, this order and the diversities of different arrange-
ments of sounds are made plain through *figurae*.[18]

Preexistent *materia*, expressed by *figurae*, arranged in, and identified as
modes of movement, and further organized in terms of increments—all
concepts prepared by centuries of use and discussion—were given new
conceptual force, particularly by the translation of Aristotle's *Physics*.
All were exemplified in music, both in writing concerning music as
well as through the *figurae* of music notation. In particular, two powerful constructs were exemplified within the discipline of music. First,
Aristotle's conceptualization of process in terms of his *theoria* model,
presented in the first book of the *Metaphysics*, which finds exemplification not only in the *Physics* but in his other treatises, such as the *Poetics*.
This process model begins with a decisive beginning, such as an important question or an action, and proceeds, step by step, to an equally
decisive conclusion. *Theoria* was exemplified as music composition,
namely the *conductus*.[19] The example that follows illustrates three of
the new conceptual forces under consideration in the first half of the
13th century, namely, preexistent *materia* (*Quo*), a composition with an
emphasized beginning, followed by step by step process to a differentiated conclusion (Aristotle's model structure, *theoria*), and contrary
motion delineated within the *Physics*, in which two intentionalities
proceeding from two different sources of movement may be brought
to resolution within motion and time.[20] Example XII (in chapter IV)
terms such as *simplex* (*figura*), *modus*, as well as the concepts of *proprietas* and *perfectio*, dealing with the actualization of potential properties inherent within an organism such as animal or, especially, human
being, emphasized within the *Physics* of Aristotle in its Latin translation, became clear—even on the face of the page—to everyone, within
the *figurae* of music notation:

But musical example was a powerful representational force because
it could be applied to learning itself, and to life. "Life" as it is lived on
a day to day basis begins anew at the start of the day and proceeds one
moment at a time until one retires at the end of a day. Furthermore, the
conclusion of a day may not be what one might have expected at its beginning, but rather, quite the contrary. Simplistic and obvious though

this model may seem, its conceptualization and reduction to verbal analysis gave control through articulation to the model, and also made it possible to apply it to many different, yet related, situations. The *theoria* model could be applied, for example, to the process of scientific experimentation in which one asks a leading question, proceeds, one experiment after the other, to a conclusion that may be the opposite of what one could have predicted at the onset. One could also apply the model to music composition, and actually hear, as well as see, through music notational *figurae,* the decisive attributes of beginning, incremental process, and conclusion or cadence, with contrary motion, point against point, note against note, all the way through to the end. Music made incipit, process, resolution, continuity and measure, potential and realization, plain.

NOTES

1. Amos Funkenstein noted in his *Theology and the Scientific Imagination from the Middle Ages to the Seventeenth Century* (Princeton, 1996) that the connections and separations between areas of learning may be the least comprehensible of cultural qualities from one geographical or temporal educational civilization compared to another.

2. *Secularization* is a comparatively recent concept, referring to burials outside of church yards. The medieval concept of *secular canon,* though an ambiguous concept, certainly does not have the connotations of the term "secular" as it may be understood today. One can, rather, speak of holy places, such as the cathedral; holy (feast) days, such as Christmas and Easter; as well as days dedicated for some reason to specific saints, holy people—all Christian believers are in some sense holy and should strive for holiness—but "holiness" is not one aspect of a contrast-pair or duality, nor does it necessarily invoke a direct opposite. Dualities do exist, such as that mentioned in Psalm I: "Blessed is the man that walketh not in the counsel of the ungodly . . . but his delight is in the law of the Lord . . . the ungodly are not so, but are like the chaff that the wind blows away . . . for the Lord knows the way of the righteous, but the way of the ungodly shall perish." But this certainly does not present the contrast-pair, "sacred-secular," but rather "godly-ungodly."

3. Troubadour/*trouvère* composers are cases in point where both dichotomies—between "sacred" and "secular" as well as "intellectual" and "non-intellectual"—are inappropriate. Again, historical situations of the past often defy our intuitive responses. On the other hand, intuition may appear to us to be most persuasive.

4. The content of textbooks in the Middle Ages differs as well from what is expected today.

5. There is much precedent for this. Both Plato and Aristotle, in bringing out what they themselves to be of particular importance, most often employ a music example to make that point clear. For example, in the *Phaedo,* in his

discussion of *harmonia* and the soul, Plato uses a the image of lyre/harp to make his point clear. The translation of the *Phaedo* into Latin during the middle years of the 12th century was followed by the image of harps appearing within literary works, on frescos, and in paintings, particular during the 14th century, as Howard Mayer Brown has documented in his catalogue "The Corpus of Trecento Pictures with Musical Subject Matter," in *Imago musicae, International Yearbook for Music Iconography* I (1984), part I, 189–243. For a discussion of the reception of Plato's *Phaedo* in the Middle Ages and its influence on the Latin-reading community, including, for example, Petrarch, see van Deusen, "The Harp and the Soul: The Image of the Harp and Trecento Reception of Plato's *Phaedo*," in *The Harp and the Soul: Essays in Medieval Music* (New York, 1989), pp. 384–416.

6. Several of the earliest complete sources containing notated music for the mass liturgy (*graduale*) as well as the offices (*antiphonale*) are available in the series *Paléographie musicale* (PalMus): compare sources from the end of the 9th century through the early 11th century, Codex 239 of the Library of Laon (PalMus series 1:11 [Tournai, 1909]), Chartres, Codex 47 (PalMus series 1:11 [Tournai, 1912]), Einsiedeln, Codex 121 (PalMus series 1:4 [Tournai, 1884]), St. Gall Codex 339 (PalMus series 1:1 [1889]), Paris, National Library Codex 903 from St. Yrieix, France (PalMus series 1:13 [1925]), both for relatively "heightening" (that is, high) tones correspond to relative highness on the manuscript page, as well as the thesis that notational *figurae* not only indicate and individuate sound in terms of tone but also indicate geographical region from whence they come. The series *Paléographie musicale*, produced anonymously by the monks of Solesme in France, illustrates two factors: (a) "anonymous" production is not circumstantial, fortuitous, or improvisatory (as has been maintained concerning the origin and development of *cantus*), and (b) the series is indicative of an increased interest in the study of the Middle Ages that resulted as well in the large-scale editions of texts such as Migne, *Patrologiae latina,* and the *Analecta hymnica* series of texts and manuscript concordances, as well as in editions and translations of writings concerning music during the course of the 20th century.

7. The list is partial, in approximate chronological order, also focusing on priorities delineated in this chapter.

8. The term *differentiae* would become even more important with the Latin translation and reception of the logical works of Aristotle, particularly the *Posterior Analytics* (by Robert Grosseteste, second generation, 13th century), but it is already used with particular emphasis by Abelard. *Differentia* has long continuity as an important expression, as we see, within the discipline of music, since it articulates what it is that a *figura* accomplishes in terms of identification; and how differing *figurae* indicate distinctions between various ways of moving. This feature, as Guido of Arezzo pointed out, can be likened to differences between groups of people based on geographical area of origin, since they all move differently. Their gait gives them away.

9. *Micrologus*, ed. pp. 150ff.: a passage that received much response, for example, from Johannes Affligimensis, ed. CSM l, 110; and in the early 14th century by Jacobus of Liege, *Speculum* 6, 92. See also Example XI in chapter IV,

in which differences between ways of moving, *modi,* are indicated by human *figurae* doing things and playing instruments. All of the components of these illustrations are *figurae*: human figures, gestural *figurae, instrumenta,* alongside music notational *figurae.* These features illustrate what varied and diverse *figurae* do, what they indicate, and why they are important.

10. Some recent studies have related the discipline of music to grammar—an obvious relationship, as Augustine points out, since both employ the same *materia,* namely, sound.

11. This was still true in Mozart's time. One of the characters in his opera buffa *Cosi fan tutte* is the Philosopher.

12. John Murdoch stated that the *Physics* received more commentary attention than any other work of Aristotle; cf. "Infinity and Continuity," in *Cambridge History of Later Medieval Philosophy,* p. 565. See also Albert Zimmermann, *Verzeichnis ungedruckter Kommentare zur Metaphysik und Physik des Aristoteles aus der Zeit von etwa 1250–1350* (Leiden, 1971) gives some impression of the vastness of the influence of Aristotle's *Metaphysics* and *Physics.* The two works provided an arsenal of topics, terms, and tools to deal with the substance of the world, both seen and unseen.

13. *Habitus,* defined by Cicero as "way of life," is an important concept for Quintilian and for thinkers throughout the Middle Ages in relation to discussion of where does *habitus* begin? Is a "way of life" intrinsic or practiced until it becomes a "second nature" or "habit"? Not only did the term gain new pungency with the translation of Aristotle's *Metaphysics* and *De anima,* but it has reappeared recently.

14. See Augustine's commentary on Psalm 57 (58), 2, quoted by Robert Grosseteste in his treatise *De cessatione legalium,* p. 37, a treatise that deals directly with the question of laws that are either "timed" or "untimed," that is, of eternal validity, *ultra mensuram;* cf. van Deusen, "*Ubi Lex*? Robert Grosseteste's Discussion of Law, Letter, and Time and its Musical Exemplification," in *Theology and Music at the Early University,* pp. 19–36.

15. Aristotle, in his treatise on "soulish substance," *De anima,* designates this increment as an "ensouled body," the contained "body" separated out from a generality of substance, and identifiable.

16. The concept of "surface" arbitrates as well this differentiation between "*plana musica*" or "*ad omnem mensurabilem musicam,*" cf. Aristotle, *Physics,* Book IV.4 (2/2a20); Hence the place or surface of a thing is the innermost motionless boundary of what contains it . . . for this reason, place is thought to be a kind of surface, and as it were, a vessel, that is, a container of the thing. Further, a place is coincident with the thing, for boundaries are coincident with the bounded. For a more thorough discussion, see van Deusen, "*Planus, cantus planus*: The Theological Background of a Significant Concept," in *Cantus planus,* Papers Read at the Sixth Meeting of the International Musicological Society Study Group, Eger, Hungary, 1993, 2 vols. (Budapest, 1995), I, pp. 13ff.

17. The movements of natures are easier to describe than the nature of movement, according to Aristotle, cf. *Physics,* cited above. It is easier to identify, for example, differences in movement between an elephant and an ant (the movements of nature), then to describe the nature of movement itself.

18. The footnotes in Erich Reimer's edition of Johannes de Garlandia's treatise indicate how this common conceptual vocabulary of *plana, mensurabilis, de longitudine et brevitate, modus soni, organum, per figuras, per modos precedit, de omni genere figurarum,* is employed by the group of Anonymous IV, Franco, Lambertus, and others.

19. It would seem that the entire 13th century was occupied, one way or the other, with an attempt to understand Aristotle's concept of *theoria,* as seen also by the difficulty with which it is discussed in *Cambridge History of Later Medieval Philosophy,* especially in chapters 34 and 35 ("The Reception and Interpretation of Aristotle's Ethics" and "Happiness: The Perfection of Man," both by Georg Wieland), pp. 657–686. But Aristotle uses the term carefully, and sparingly, for a model of process. The concept, emphasized in the *Physics,* also carries the connotation of directionality, trajectory motion, and leadership (*ductus*) from beginning to end. As a measure of the importance of an understanding of *theoria,* especially during the early years of the 13th century, the Greek *theoria* was replaced with the Latin *ductus,* rather than simply appropriating the Greek term. See van Deusen, "Ductus, Tractus, Conductus: The Intellectual Context of a Musical Genre, " in *Theology and Music,* pp. 37–53; as well as "A Theory of Composition and its Influence," pp. 127–145.

20. Florence, Biblioteca Laurentiana Ms 29.1, facsimile ed. Luther A. Dittmer, 2 vols., publications of Medieval Musical Manuscripts, 10 (Brooklyn, New York, no date). The manuscript provides *exempla* for the most important concepts of the 13th century and contains the largest repository of *conductus* texts for which a case can be made for the authorship of Philip the Chancellor, whose office constituted a liaison between the episcopal see of Notre Dame and the emerging theology faculty of the University of Paris. Both institutions were at the time undergoing a period of nascence and growth. See van Deusen, "On the Usefulness of Music: Motion, Music, and the Thirteenth-century Reception of Aristotle's *Physics,*" *Viator,* 29 (1998), 167–187.

8

Music at the Forefront of Science: The Usefulness of Medieval Music

Historical musicology as a historical discipline as it emerged near the beginning of the 20th century has written a narrative indicative of the major historiographical models of the 20th century. One can trace, in the textbooks produced by this new discipline, the major historiographical models as they have appeared first in some cases in art history and architecture ("form" applied to music in the 1920s, the priority of "style");[1] evolutionary biological metaphors (organic, genetic "evolution" as an explanation for music composition); the notion of "schools," introduced by, and more appropriate to history of art, but taken up then as an historiographical model by the university study of history.[2] Nineteenth-century conceptualizations of "genius" resulting in a view of the composer as "inspired" to "create" great, autonomous works has also clearly influenced a 20th-century view of the development of music history presented both within undergraduate textbooks (which have had remarkable staying power—and outstanding commercial advantage) as well as more specialized articles within the emerging field of musicology.[3] On the other hand, a concept of folklore—and the originating potential of ordinary people particularly from remote places as capable of extraordinary creative activity largely through improvisation (i.e., happenstance)—has also influenced a narrative explanation for the relatively sudden emergence of both *cantus* and the means to present it in music notation *figurae*.[4]

All of these models that emerged during the course of the 20th century have been greeted with both enthusiasm as well as critical distance. They have all appeared to be worthy of acceptance, achieving persuasive force as an explanatory vehicle during the course of the 20th century. However, "form," "schools," "folk culture," a free-wheeling, ill-defined concept of "improvisation" that corresponded to late 19th and 20th-century notions of "freedom"—all these concepts have

20th-century conceptual origins. When applied to music history, these models have also solved the problem of teaching the history of Western music with very little recourse to its basis and educational system within developing Christianity on the continent of Europe and in Christendom in general. Western medieval music, as a constituent and important illustrative discipline within an educational milieu that culminated in the study of the nature of God, defied a contemporary 20th-century separation of faith and education. It was necessary to find other explanatory models within a recognizable narrative.[5]

These models, however, have little to do with the conceptual basis of medieval music. Music, in the Middle Ages, and certainly much thereafter, was placed at the forefront of scientific investigation and discussion. Much as "music history" has reflected, one text after the other, the paradigms of the 20th century, so music reflected intellectual priorities, one after the other, of the many centuries under discussion here. Music also, as many such as Augustine, Guido of Arezzo, Robert Grosseteste, and Roger Bacon all pointed out, made abstractions plain. Music was a ministry discipline, with the opportunity and challenge to present the realities of the world around us, and of life itself.

These realities have remained much the same, and ways of both expressing them and dealing with them recur. One is often reminded of the priorities identified as such in the Middle Ages, as for example, in a recent newspaper article concerning "dark matter, which is thought to comprise almost all of the material in the universe" (both seen and unseen, as the article goes on to mention). "Without dark matter, the universe does not make sense."[6] In fact, our discussion of medieval mental civilization and music's place within it opened with just this concept of preexistent substance, both seen, as well as unseen, as a basis for differentiation and individuation, defined by characteristic *figurae*. This, now returning as a hypothetical construct for conceptualizing the world in which we live, is one of many modern constructs shared with medieval thought civilization. These often anonymous writers are dealing with difficult questions that required muscular thinking and rigorous dialogue. Other issues that are recognizable from medieval thought culture include: (a) the *theoria* model, earnestly debated as the result of the translation of Aristotle's *Metaphysics* and *Physics*; (b) the question of *habitus*, or propensities that could be ingrained or acquired by cultivation; (c) differentiation between event and process; and (d) the useful model of contrary motion to describe dialectical encounter, resulting in conclusion and reconciliation within motion and the passage of time. Furthermore, they have retained their importance today. Though perhaps expressed differently, and answered differently, the basic principles are similar if not the same. In other words, far from a rather childish atmosphere of medieval fantasy that is sometimes projected by both the media and "common opinion," the questions asked, the debates that ensued, and some of the answers that these dialogues produced are all astonishingly relevant. These topics deal, as we have seen, with the nature of the world, with its possibilities of infinite differentiation, relationships between these different things, and their characteristic movements, as well as how to measure all of this and communicate these analyses in a cogent, logical manner. Material, measurement, interpretation, and communication are all goals.

How then do ideas find expression and, sooner or later, become accepted? Art historian Ernst Gombrich wrote in several contexts that the entry of concepts into the mainstream of a mental culture might be more like coffee brewing somewhere: one is aware of the aroma first. Accompanying questions include: What are illustrations, examples, analogies "good for"? What is the connection between illustration and the material itself, between sound and the *figurae* that indicate this unseen substance? Is it not true that sound cannot be transformed into anything other than itself, that music notation is quite different from the sound it indicates, as a letter of the alphabet differs from the sound of a vowel? What is the relationship between the sound of one's voice as one speaks and the alphabetical letters indicating these words on a page (a relationship that also exists in similar ways between pictorial illustration and text)? Such are questions that were—and are— pertinent to music within its medieval thought context.[7] They are still with us today, perhaps most consciously in what has become known as ethnomusicology, dealing primarily with oral music traditions.

The exceptional benefit of music as a component of this mental enterprise was that in order to understand the point that was being made, one needed to actually *do* it.[8] To learn by doing, according to Augustine, makes all the difference. Music, therefore, constituted a powerful bridge, not only to invisible substance generally, with all of its potential and possibilities of actualization, but to life itself, since one learned most not only by speaking of activities and properties but by engaging in them. Augustine also thought that by so doing, one generated even more interest for the activity in question—that the more one made music, the greater the appetite for it. Augustine, and many others, realized that a reciprocity of reflection over phenomena and life experience could be achieved in a particular way within the study and experience of music; that writing concerning music could be—and is—experiential, explanatory, and paradigmatic.[9]

The medieval priority of inner, invisible substance made the unseen comprehensible. We know this, perhaps, as "spirituality," and as a differing order of "thing" than "materiality," or "matter"; but medieval mental civilization consistently made no such distinction. The fact remains that even in affluent, postindustrial society, there remains a desire or appetite for unseen, invisible "capital" that cannot be satisfied by external, visible "goods." The entire question of inner values, and of goods or value itself, considered in its most basic manifestation—as well as how to consider its absence or presence—brings up medieval questions of greatest importance, exemplified by the music of the Middle Ages.

NOTES

1. "Form" is pervasive in both music history textbooks as well as music pedagogy, although, derived from architectural parlance, it was not accepted without some protest, since buildings remain in place and music does not. The notion of "style" has been continuously contested, for example, by Ernst Gombrich, who was highly suspicious of any such generalizing concepts.

2. For a cogent summary of the impact of the historiographical model on the discipline of history, more importantly, medieval studies, see William J. Courtenay, "Schools and Schools of Thought in the Twelfth Century," in *Mind Matters. Studies in Medieval and Early Modern History in Honor of Marcia Colish*, eds. Cary J. Nederman, Nancy van Deusen, and E. Ann Matter (Turnhout, 2009), pp. 13–46.

3. "Great Men, Great Works" as pillars upon which to hang the narrative of music history has been a common method of organization within music history textbooks. See the useful "Bibliographical Note" concluding Marcia L. Colish's *Medieval Foundations of the Western Intellectual Tradition, 400–1400* (New Haven, 1997), pp. 364–369.

4. Based on a misunderstanding of Herder's writing and hypotheses, as well as of 20th-century priorities applied to a writer of the 18th century, writing against a background of medieval Latin–language-based concepts and educational system, a view of poetic lyricism emanating from "uncorrupted" country people can be perceived as a explanatory force in, for example, Zoltán Kodály, *Hungarian Folkmusic,* first published in Hungarian in 1939, with an English translation, as well as Albert Lord, *The Singer of Tales,* which apparently influenced Leo Treitler in his "Homer and Gregory," in which he applies this prevalent, at that time, view of "folk creativity" to the emergence of *cantus,* namely a folk culture, "improvisational model."

5. Textbooks, particularly within the North American university education (particularly during the second half of the 20th century, encouraged by burgeoning undergraduate classes as the result of the considerable educational opportunities offered to returning military service personnel), have appeared to be of great commercial value both to author as well as publisher due to the large music programs particularly within the "land-grant universities" of the Midwestern states within the United States. These texts have been reissued without considerable change during the course of the late 20th century,

instilling such priorities as "The Notre Dame School" or "Burgundian School" of composition, as well as the ubiquitous notion of "form" into generations of undergraduates within North American education.

6. *Los Angeles Times,* March 20, 2000, "Darkest Puzzle of the Cosmos." This article dealt with "dark, impacted, matter," which, as the writer states, makes up more than 90 percent of the universe—in other words, limitless, preexistent substance/material/*silva*. See also David Filkin, *Stephen Hawking's Universe: The Cosmos Explained* (New York, 1997).

7. One can trace an immense literature on this topic throughout the Middle Ages; the topic gained importance, as one might imagine, during the early university (13th century).

8. "Performance" as a term is deliberately avoided in this context, since a spectator, concert connotation would have been foreign during the periods we have been addressing. Modern concert attitudes in which "performance" is understood as a rather rigid separation between "audience" and "performer" were not common in the Middle Ages; rather, the separation between "audience" and "performer" is a comparatively recent distinction (i.e., the second half of the 18th century).

9. Exemplification within medieval music, as well as the mental context that surrounds it, provides a link to the musical cultures of the world. Cf. Steven M. Friedson, *Dancing Prophets: Musical Experience in Tumbuka Healing* (Chicago, 1996). Music, then and now, in many parts of the world also exemplifies community as a concept—a concept that brings together particularity, relationship, and motion.

Editions: Music to Sing

In Epiphania Domini
Ad Vesperas Super Psalmos
[Antiphona]   Paris 1236, f. 59

Te - cum prin - ci   -   pi - um.

Versiculus   f. 59

Re - ges thar - sis   et   in - su - le.

Ad Magnificat   f. 59
[Antiphona]

Ve - nit   lu - men   tu - um, hie - ru - sa - - lem, et glo - - -

ri - a do - mi - ni   su - per   te   or - ta   est,

et   am - bu - la - bunt gen - tes   in   lu - mi - ne   tu - o,

al - le - lu - ia.   Se - cu - lo - rum   a - men.
[Ad Matutinas]
Invitatorium   f. 59v

Cri   -   stus ap - pa - ru - it   no - bis,   ve   -   ni - te

ad - o - re - - - mus.

Ps.Ve - ni - te...   Iu - bi - le - mus e - - - i.

Edition I and II: Service of Epiphany, Nevers Cathedral, ca. 1120, edition from manuscripts Paris, National Library, new collection of Latin manuscripts 1235 (a *graduale* containing music and texts for the Proper of the Mass), 1236 (an *antiphonale* containing music and texts for the Offices), cf. van Deusen, *Music at Nevers Cathedral: Principal Sources of Medieval Chant*, 2 vols. (Binningen, Switzerland, 1980), II.147–179. Used by permission of the publisher.

[In I Nocturno]

Edition I and II: (continued)

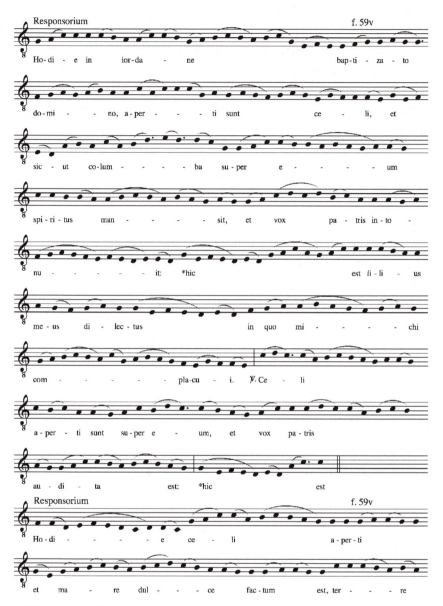

Edition I and II: (continued)

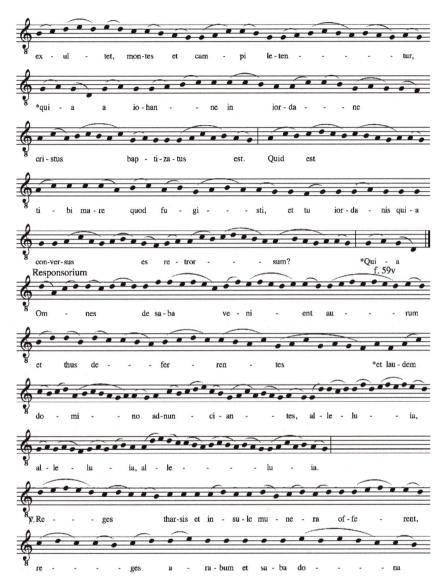

Edition I and II: (continued)

ad - - - du - - - cent   *Et lau - dem

[In II Nocturno]

Antiphona   f. 60

Om - nes ter - ra ad - o - ret te et psal - lat ti - bi,

psal - mum di - cat no - mi - ni tu - o, do - mi - ne.

se - cu - lo - rum a - men. Ps. Iu - bi - la - te.

Antiphona   f. 60

Re - ges thar - sis et in - su - le mu - ne - ra of - fe - rent

re - gi do - mi - no. Se - cu - lo - rum a - men.

Ps. De - us iu - di - ci - um.

Antiphona   f. 60

Om - nes gen - tes quas - cum - que fe - ci - sti ve - ni - ent,

et ad - o - ra - bunt co - ram te, do - mi - ne.

Edition I and II: (continued)

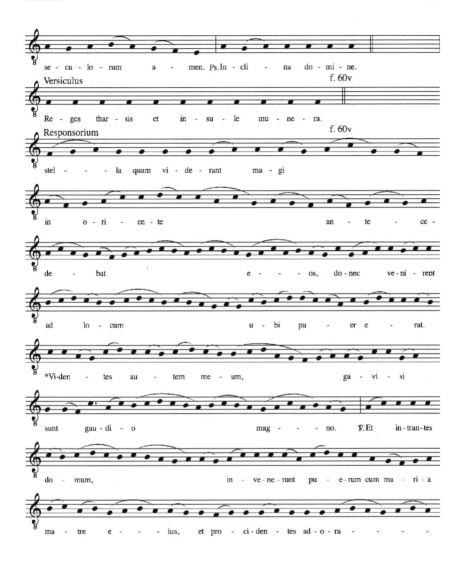

se - cu - lo - rum a - - men. Ps. In - cli - - na do - mi - ne.

Versiculus   f. 60v

Re - ges thar - sis et in - su - le mu - ne - ra.

Responsorium   f. 60v

stel - - - - la quam vi - de - rant ma - gi

in o - ri - en - te an - te - ce -

de - bat e - - - os, do - nec ve - ni - rent

ad lo - cum u - bi pu - er e - - rat.

*Vi - den - tes au - tem me - um, ga - vi - si

sunt gau - di - o mag - - - no. ℣. Et in - tran-tes

do - mum, in - ve - ne - runt pu - e - rum cum ma - ri - a

ma - tre e - - - ius, et pro - ci - den - tes ad - o - ra - - - -

Edition I and II: (continued)

ve - runt e - - - - um.   *Vi-den - tes

Responsorium

In - ter - ro - ga - bat ma - ges he - ro - des:

quod sig - num vi - di - stis   su - per na - tum

re - - - gem? Stel-lam mag - nam ful - gen - - - tem, cu - - - ius

splen - dor il - lu - mi - nat   mun - - - - - dum,

*et nos cog - no - vi - - mus et ve - ni - mus,

ad - o - ra - re   do - mi - num.

℣. Ma - gi   ve - ni-unt ab o - ri - en - te,

in - qui - ren - tes fa - ci - em do - mi - ni   et di - - - cen - tes.

*Et nos

Edition I and II: (continued)

Edition I and II: (continued)

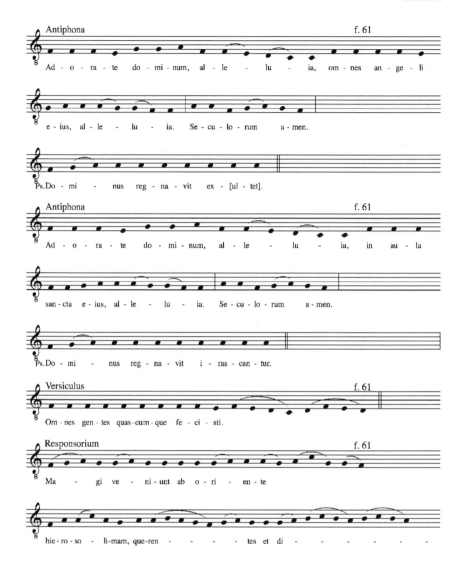

Edition I and II: (continued)

Edition I and II: (continued)

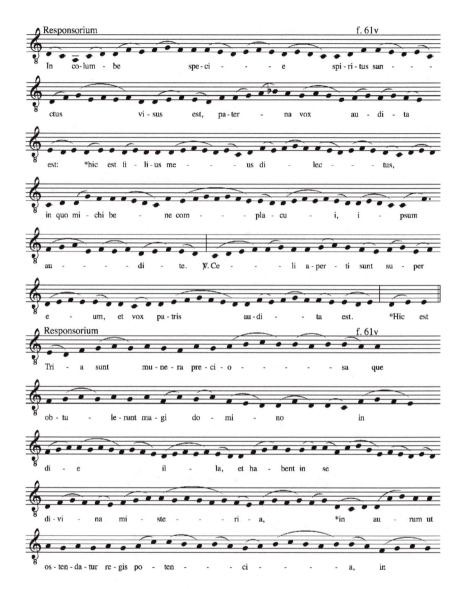

Edition I and II: (continued)

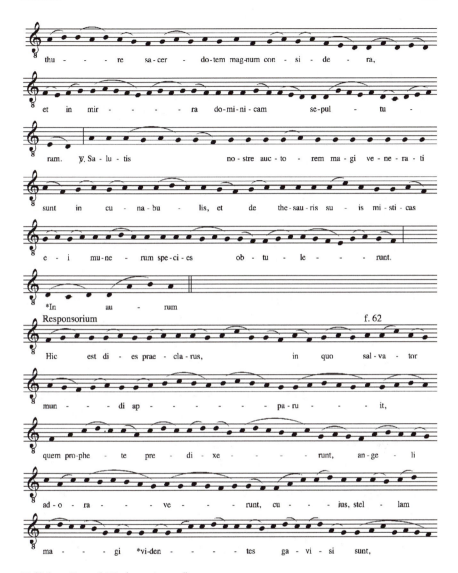

Edition I and II: (continued)

et mu - ne - ra e - i ob - - - tu - - le - - - runt.

℣. Et in-tran-tes do - mum. *Vi-den - - - - tes

Responsorium f. 62

Vi - den - tes stel - lam ma - - - gi, ga - - vi - si sunt

gau - di - o mag - no, *et in - tran - tes do - mum,

in - ve - ne - runt pu - e - - - rum cum ma - ri - a ma - - tre e - ius,

et pro - ci - den - - - tes ad - o - ra - ve - runt e - um,

et a - per - - - tis the - - sau - ris su - - - is

ob - tu - le - - - runt e - i mu - ne - - ra, au - rum,

thus et mir - ram. ℣. Stel - la

quam vi - de - rant ma - gi in o - ri - en - te an - te - ce - de - bat

e - os, us - - - que - dum ve - ni - ens sta - ret su - pra

Edition I and II: (continued)

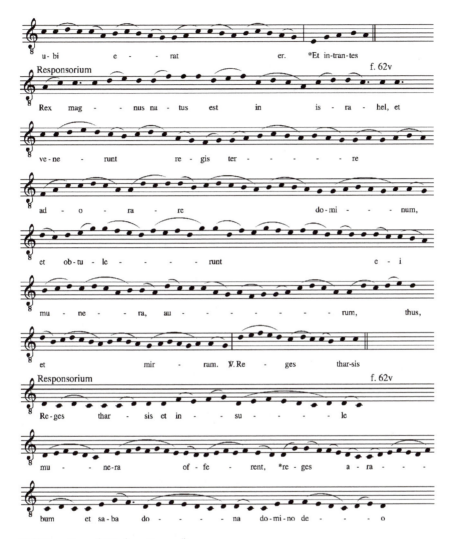

u - bi   e - rat   er. *Et in-tran-tes

Responsorium   f. 62v

Rex mag - - nus na - tus   est   in   is - ra - hel, et

ve - ne - runt   re - gis ter - - - - - re

ad - o - ra - re   do - mi - - - num,

et   ob - tu - le - - - runt   e - i

mu - ne - ra,   au - - - - - - - rum,   thus,

et   mir - ram. ℣. Re - ges   thar-sis

Responsorium   f. 62v

Re - ges   thar - sis et in - - su - - - - le

mu - - ne - ra   of - fe - rent, *re - ges   a - ra - - -

bum   et sa - ba   do - - - - na   do - mi - no de - - - o

Edition I and II: (continued)

ad - - - du - - - - cent. ℣. Et ad - o - ra - - - - bunt e - um

om - nes re - ges, om - nes gen - tes ser - - - - vi - ent

e - - - - - i.
Responsorium: A presentis festi   *Re - ges
In Matutinis laudibus [Antiphona]   f. 63

An - te lu - ci - - - fe - rum ge - ni - tus, et an - te se - cu - la

do - mi - - nus, sal - va - tor no - ster ho - di - e mun - do

ap - pa - ru - it. Se - cu - lo - rum a - men.

Antiphona   f. 63

Tri - a sunt mu - ne - ra que ob - tu - le - runt ma - gi

do - mi - no, au - rum, thus et mir - ram, fi - li - o de - i,

re - gi mag - no, al - le - lu - ia. Se - cu - lo - rum a - men.

Antiphona   f. 63

A - per - tis the - sau - ris su - is, ob - - - - tu - le - runt ma - gi

do - mi - no au - rum, thus et mi - ram, al - le - - - lu - ia.

Edition I and II: (continued)

Edition I and II: (continued)

Edition I and II: (continued)

Edition I and II: (continued)

li - ne - is pro - pe - ran - do ve - ni - te.

Rex:

O vos scri - be, in - ter - ro - ga - ti di - ci - te, si quid de

hoc pu - e - ro scrip - tum vi - de - ri - tis in li - bris.

Semiste:

Vi - di - mus, do - mi - ne, in pro - phe - ta - rum li - ne - is,

quod ma - ni - fe - ste scrip - tum est:

Chorus:

Beth - le - em, non e - ris mi - ni - ma in prin - ci - pi - bus

iu - da, ex te e - nim ex - i - et dux, qui re - gat

po - pu - lum me - um is - ra - hel, i - pse e - nim sal - vum

fa - ci - et po - pu - lum su - um a pec - ca - tis e - o - rum.

Edition I and II: (continued)

Rex:

Re - gem, quem que - ri - tis?

Magi:

Il - lum na - tum es - se.

Rex:

Si il - lum reg - na - re

Rex:

I - te et de pu - e - ro

Magi:

Ec - ce stel - la in o - ri - en - te.

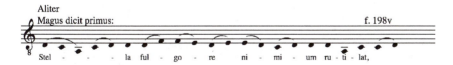

Aliter

Magus dicit primus: f. 198v

Stel - la ful - go - re ni - mi - um ru - ti - lat,

Edition I and II: (continued)

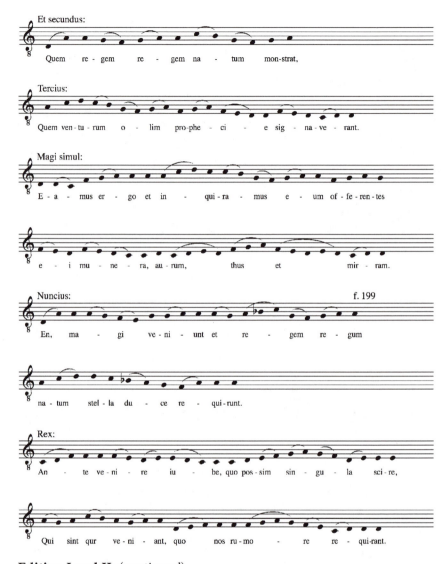

Et secundus:
Quem re - gem re - gem na - tum mon-strat,

Tercius:
Quem ven - tu - rum o - lim pro-phe - ci - e sig - na - ve - rant.

Magi simul:
E - a - mus er - go et in - qui-ra - mus e - um of - fe - ren-tes

e - i mu - ne - ra, au-rum, thus et mir - ram.

Nuncius: f. 199
En, ma - gi ve - ni - unt et re - gem re - gum

na - tum stel - la du - ce re - qui-runt.

Rex:
An - te ve - ni - re iu - be, quo pos - sim sin - gu - la sci - re,

Qui sint qur ve - ni - ant, quo nos ru - mo - re re - qui-rant.

Edition I and II: (continued)

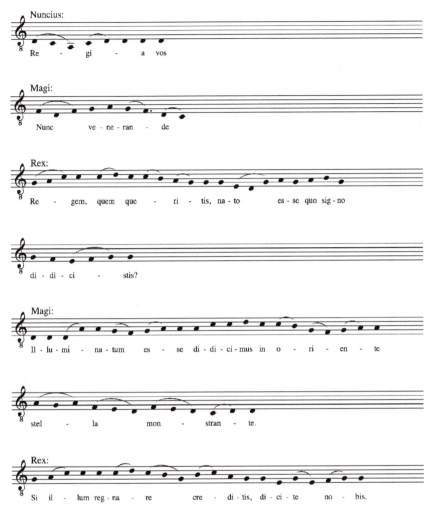

Edition I and II: (continued)

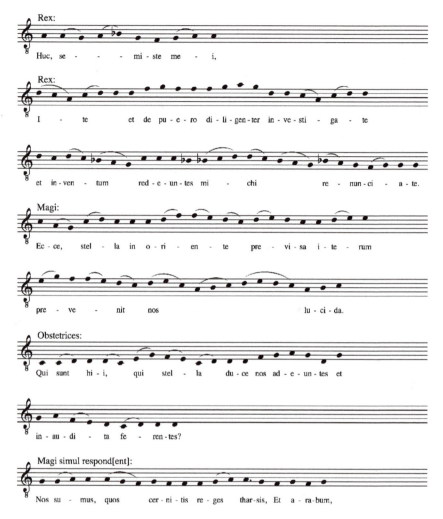

Edition I and II: (continued)

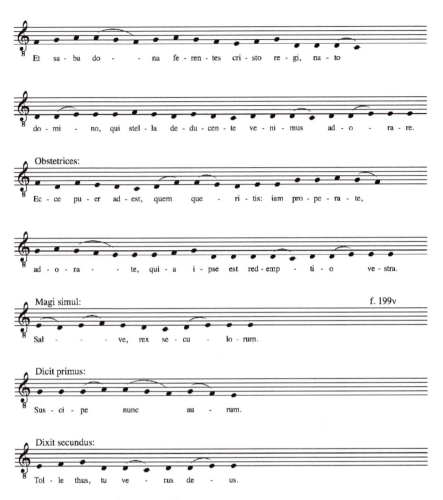

Edition I and II: (continued)

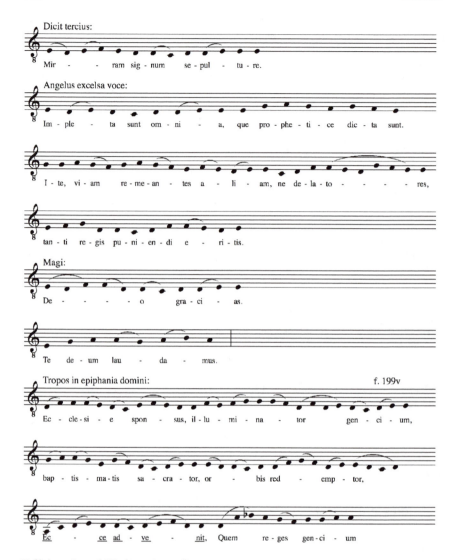

Edition I and II: (continued)

cum mu - ne - ri - bus mi - sti - cis hie - ro - so - li - mam

re - qui - runt, di - cen - tes: u - bi est qui na - tus est,

Do - mi - na - tor do - - mi - - - nus? Vi - di - mus stel - lam e - ius

in o - ri - en - te, et ag - no - vi - mus re - gem

re - - - gum es - se na - tum, Et reg - num, Cu - - - i

so - li de - be - tur ho - - - - - nor, laus et iu - bi - la - ci - o,

Et po - te - stas. Ps. De - us iu - di - ci - um.

Ec - - - ce ad - ve - - - nit.

f. 199v

Al - le - lu - - - i - a.

[Prosa]

Psal - le, tur - ba ca - no - ra fra - trum, dul - ci - a nunc can - ti - ca
me - lo - di - ma - ta do - mi - no - que iu - ga rith - mi - ca,

Edition I and II: (continued)

Edition I and II: (continued)

f. 200

quo ma - nent gau - di - a si - ne fi - ne ma - nen - ci - a.

Al - le - lu - ia.

Prosa

E - pi - pha - ni - am do - mi - no ca - na - mus glo - ri - o - sam,

Qua pro - lem de - i ve - re ma - gi ad - o - rant.

Im - men - sam cal - de - i cu - ius per - se - qui ve - ne - ran - tur
Quem cun - cta pro - phe - ta ce - ci - ne - re ven - tu - rum gen - tes

po - ten - ci - am,
ad sal - van - das.

Cu - ius ma - ie - stas i - ta est in - cli - na - ta,
An - te se - cu - la qui de - us et tem - po - ra,

ut as - su - me - ret ser - vi for - mam,
ho - mo fac - tus est in ma - ri - a.

Ba - la - am de quo va - ti - ci - nans,
Et con - frin - get du - cum ag - mi - na

Ex - i - bit ex ia - cob ru - ti - lans, in - quit, stel - la
Re - gi - on - nis mo - ab ma - xi - ma po - ten - ci - a.

Edition I and II: (continued)

Edition I and II: (continued)

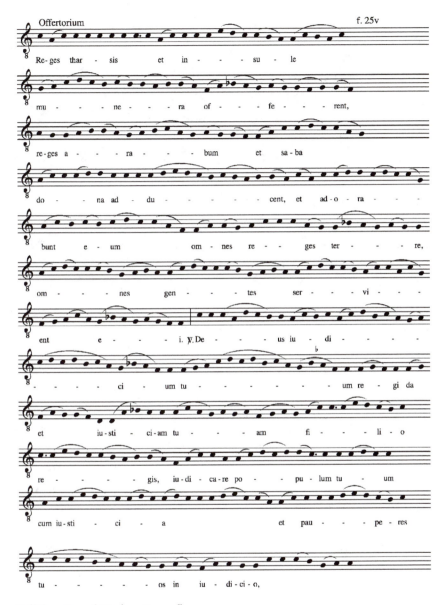

Edition I and II: (continued)

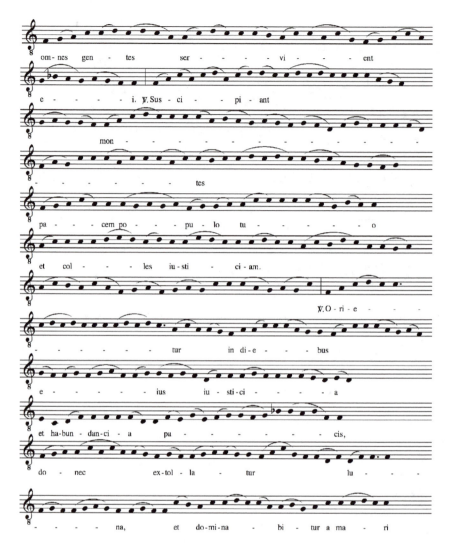

Edition I and II: (continued)

Edition I and II: (continued)

Edition I and II: (continued)

Edition I and II: (continued)

Edition I and II: (continued)

Edition I and II: (continued)

Edition I and II: (continued)

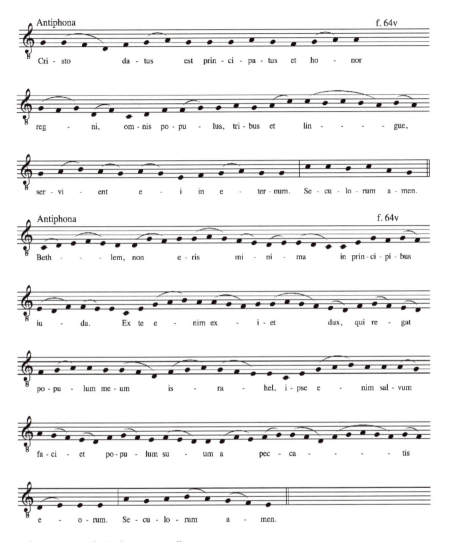

Edition I and II: (continued)

Edition III: Responsory, with melisma <u>Fabrice</u> <u>mundi</u>

<u>Fabricator mundi</u>: <u>Fabrice mundi</u>
Use of the vocabulary of <u>Timaeus</u> <u>latinus</u> within liturgical music
(from van Deusen, <u>Music</u> <u>at</u> <u>Nevers</u> <u>Cathedral</u>: <u>Principal</u> <u>Sources</u> <u>of</u> <u>Medieval</u> <u>Chant</u>, 2 vols
[Binningen, Switzerland, 1980], II: 13)

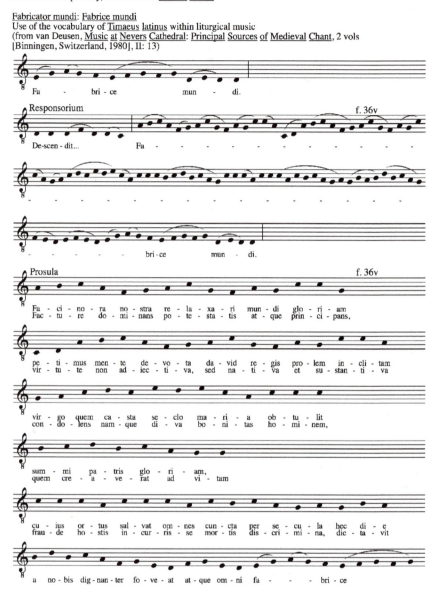

Edition III: Responsory (from the Office Hours) with melisma *Fabrice mundi* and texts *facinora nostra, facture dominans*, with vocabulary and subject matter references to the Latin *Timaeus* (author's edition).

Edition IV: Sequence: <u>Promissa mundi gaudia</u>

Edition IV: Sequence, *Promissa mundi gaudia*.

Edition IV: (continued)

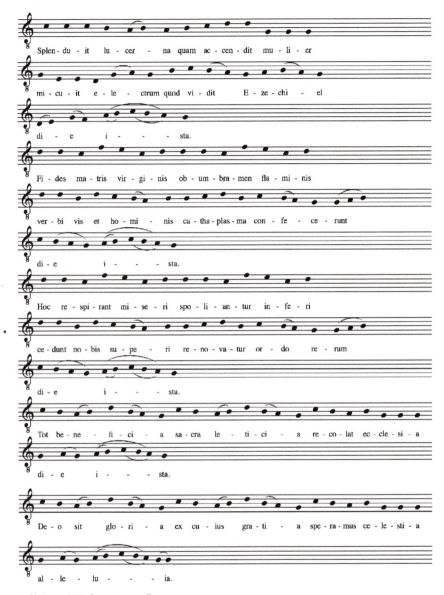

Splen-du - it lu - cer - na quam ac - cen - dit mu - li - er

mi - cu - it e - le - ctrum quod vi - dit E - ze - chi - el

di - e i - - - sta.

Fi - des ma - tris vir - gi - nis ob - um - bra - men fla - mi - nis

ver - bi vis et ho - mi - nis ca - tha - plas - ma con - fe - ce - runt

di - e i - - - sta.

Hoc re - spi - rant mi - se - ri spo - li - an - tur in - fe - ri

ce - dunt no - bis su - pe - ri re - no - va - tur or - do re - rum

di - e i - - - sta.

Tot be - ne - fi - ci - a sa - cra le - ti - ci - a re - co - lat ec - cle - si - a

di - e i - - - sta.

De - o sit glo - ri - a ex cu - ius gra - ti - a spe - ra - mus ce - le - sti - a

al - le - lu - - - ia.

Edition IV: (continued)

Glossary of Terms

alternatim: Principle of composition in which ways of moving (such as the historical, allegorical, analogical, tropological, and eschatological *modi*) alternate one with the other, according to the precedent of the Old and New Testaments; exemplified also in text/music *modi* as articulated and actualized in the *cantus*. During the course of the mass celebration, all of the musical, as well as the verbal, *modi* are alternated. This is an important principle of text-music composition throughout the Middle Ages, as well as much thereafter.

anima: Latin term meaning "mind," "soul," "intellect," "personality," "character within one expression," "unseen 'soulish substance' in an equivalent relationship with visible substance" (Aristotle, *De anima*).

armonia: Greek term translated into the Latin as *modulatio* (Chalcidius), meaning "bringing together opposing directionalities, intentionalities, or entities" (such as force and reason [Augustine]); of particular importance as a concept within the introduction of Aristotle's *Physics* in the early 13th century, as resolution (*concordancia*) of "contrary motions" within motion and time.

cantus: Often translated into English as "chant"; an important concept in the Middle Ages, implying the resource of *materia/substantia* as a repository of all of the available music/texts for both mass celebration and the offices. Sound is "shaped" in *cantus* (Augustine).

cento: Greek term translated into Latin as *punctum, puncta, pungo*: a "chunk" with perceived containment, a "manageable" piece of *materia* such as text, speech, conceptual content that could be easily retained in the memory (Quintilian); individual, self-contained modules that could be ordered (*ordo*). The concept *punctum contra punctum* retains this meaning of enclosed module, such as an individual tone set against another enclosed module, resulting in simultaneous occurrence.

copula: Coupler, joiner. An important concept due to music's function as exemplifying relationship. Apt for bringing together of separate *partes* is the basis of mastery combined with knowledge of the material with which one is working.

corpus: Containment, enclosure, delimitation of otherwise inchoate substance, as in Aristotle's concept of "ensouled body."

differentia: Inchoate, indeterminate, disorganized mass (of sound, of conceptual substance), also designated by the term *silva*, can be consciously differentiated into particular manners of moving and existence hence, multiple *differences* within general mass, indicated by *figurae* (Chalcidius commentary on the *Timaeus*); an important term for all of the sciences, as, for example, Abelard's usage (1079–1142) in terms of *differentiae* of arguments within logical discourse. *Differentiae* are important as contrasted with, and selected out of *silva*, or undifferentiated substance.

figura: One of many translations of Greek *schema*. Delineating, characteristic features that also grant individuality to each *punctum*, or chunk. There are many equivalent expressions such as *littera, instrumentum, numerus, virga, characterismos.* (All of the many translations of *schema* are united by the fact that they are all *figurae*. Important to Plato, *Timaeus latinus,* Augustine, Cassiodorus, Guido of Arezzo as the delineatory, consistent, memorable, characteristic indication of invisible properties within substance; that is, a differentiating agent within *materia-substantia* and within movement, hence useful as differentiating/delineatory agent or "instrument" within each one of the disciplines. Found in relationship to, and contrast with: varied and diverse *figurae* (*figurae variarae, characterae variarae—charivari*). Appears to be an important medieval *topos*, as well as an essential distinction that was made between a simple *figura* (*figura simplex*) that stood for itself, and an entire alphabet of *figurae*, which, in their varied diversities, indicated a whole variety of characteristics. Varied and diverse figures are also "varieties of voices" (Cicero). Just as the varied and diverse letters (*figurae*) of the alphabet present a diversity of gestures and delineations, just so the varied and diverse *figurae* are to be seen among the peoples of the world—their movements, preoccupations, languages, and habits—present the diversities of human life. This concept is useful for a medieval ethnography (to be found in the many commentaries on the book of Genesis throughout the Middle Ages), but it is also illustrated within the analogical discipline of music by the concept of figures within modes (*figurae in modis*) and the diversities of the modes (Guido of Arezzo).

firmamentum: Preexistent substance, aggregated substance, used as a foundation for further composition.

glossa ordinaria: Commentary on both Old and New Testaments by multiple authors, whose identities have not been fully established and/or connected to the portions of commentaries they authored. Culminated in, and useful for, the school curriculum of the late 12th century.

graduale: Book (or manuscript copied by hand) containing all of the *cantus* for the mass celebrations within the entire year as they vary from one service to the other. These are the *proper cantus* of the *temporale,* and for the saints' celebrations, the *sanctorale,* that is, appropriate *cantus* for the distinctive times of the entire year, day by day.

hyle: Greek term translated as the Latin *silva, materia/substancia,* eventually *cantus.* Quintilian, in writing concerning *argumenta* (V.x.33), writes of *hyle* as *materia* from which one could fashion arguments. This *materia/substantia* is the substance of sound/movement/time, divisible into types, related to how one can shape and differentiate this *materia,* thus making something out of it. In other words, one can adapt, increase, conserve, use, drive out the unworthy part, diminish, put up with, and deliberate *materia* "in several manners" (*modi*). Music composition exemplified these treatments of sound as substance in terms of "divisions," augmentation, diminution, conservation (of preexistent material). Quintilian rarely used this Greek term *hyle,* but he used it in just the manner brought out by Chalcidius in translating *hyle* into *silva.*

integumentum: A covering of hidden substance, containing movement; the concept/term is important for differentiating the allegorical "way of moving" in which intention or inner substance is deliberately hidden from superficial, hasty, careless notice.

interval: Space, also as "a space of time" or "length of time" (Cicero); interval is suggested with respect to the perception and measurement of the relationship between high and low (Martianus Capella).

Liber psalmorum: The Old Testament Book of Psalms, an important foundation not only of medieval education, but also for the understanding of the *modi,* or ways of moving, found in the biblical scriptures; a resource as well for the entire body of *cantus.* The *Liber psalmorum* was considered as an entity in the Middle Ages, the Psalter.

locus: Latin translation of the Greek *topos.* Translated into English as "commonplace," and into German as "*Gemeinplatz,*" that is, succinct statements that are self-contained and dispositive, and require no further explanation. A "place" to begin or to end an argument or a composition.

materia: Latin term. Equivalent expressions include: *substantia, natura, silva,* and *cantus. Timaeus latinus* refers to both visible *materia* as well as invisible *materia,* opaque, undifferentiated (in contrast to *differentiae*), inchoate, unlimited, a "thicket' of available resources, that is, preexistent *materia.* Can be translated into the English as "stuff."

materia/artificialis: Undifferentiated, inchoate *materia-substantia-natura* that has been worked with, fashioned, arranged, and dealt with in some way (*artificialis*). A contrast between preexistent substance or *materia* and substance that has been appropriated and worked with for some purpose. An important medieval *topos.*

melisma: Many tones paired with one or a few syllables of text, resulting in an entirely different syllable-tone relationship compared to, for example, the sequence (see Editions: Music to Sing), with its strict syllable-tone concurrence.

modulatio: Latin translation of Greek *armonia,* that is, bringing together in a well-considered, appropriate manner two completely disparate entities (such as tones). Indicates connection between particular things, most of all, *appropriate* joining (also within *ordo*).

modus: Latin term for Greek *pathos, passio, affectus* (other translations of *pathos*), manners of movement identified by and with distinguishing features (*figurae*). *Modus* also has the connotation of process and change within that process. *Modus* contains, but does not necessarily express, emotional substance, such as "dignity" (Dorian mode) or "hysterical joy" (Phrygian mode) or "quiet contentment" (Mixolydian mode).

motus: Latin term for Greek *energeia* (Aristotle *Physics*). *Physics, modus* implies motion, ways of moving, as well as the possibility that motion can be differentiated.

ordo: Order most frequently based on concept of prior/posterior, as used by Augustine in *De ordine*. *Ordo* is exemplified in the discipline of music with respect to particular tones following one after the other and accrues additional importance within Aristotle's concept of *theoria* in which, following an initial question or statement, one increment follows the other within a logical order until a conclusion is reached (*Metaphysics*, further exemplified in the *Physics, Poetics, Ethics,* and in the music of the 13th century). *Ordo* also refers to a concept of mastery since the bringing together of *partes* in an appropriate manner resulted in an effective composition. The *ordo* of the Psalms was deliberately interrupted to be reordered within the *cantus*.

pars, partes: Of eternity, of time. Identified as an "event" or "occasion" in which each part differs from the other (Cicero); *partes* are differentiated by attributes (*figurae*) or can be related to surface, confined, delimited space.

planctus: Based on the category of lamentation within the Old Testament scriptures, *planctus* introduces the concept of prior/posterior in terms of "what has been the case previously," (favorable) compared to "the present" (unfavorable).

planus, superficies: On the face or surface. A concept that achieves importance as a contrast-pair with "measurement;" *planus* vs. *mensurabilis* in a discussion of material properties within Aristotle's *Physics*.

poetica: Greek term translated into Latin as *opera*: fashioning a work (*opus*), as discussed within Aristotle's *Poetica*, in which continuous narrative continuity (plot) is measured and differentiated by increments identified by *figurae*, a structure applicable to and illustrated by music that also uses time, sound, and motion as *materia*.

proprietas, proprietates: Latin term: inherent properties or qualities; all *materia* contains, or "participates in," *proprietates* that may or may not be expressed, that is, brought to perfection; hence the term-pair *proprietas-perfectio*, indicated by delineatory *figurae*, in which the first portion of the music notational *figura* displays "property" (*proprietas*), the concluding portion *perfectio*.

pulsus: Term used by Augustine referring to enclosed "body" containing vitality or "soulish substance," that is, "enlivened enclosure." Comparable to Aristotle's "ensouled body" (*De anima*). *Pulsus,* for Augustine, makes plain the concept of the "substance of the soul" (which is "life," according to Aristotle), as well as "body," or containment within a generality of sound substance.

punctum: Latin translation of *cento;* contained *materia* (of sound, time, movement); length approximately what one could speak comfortably on one breath (Quintilian); or conceptual unity that can be retained in the memory (as in Virgil's *Aeneid,* or found in the Psalms), hence a compositional building block.

sequentia, pro sequentia (prosa): The *copula* or bond between Old Testament (*Alleluia*) and New Testament reading of the Gospel, expressing and delineating the allegorical followed by the eschatological *modi* or "ways of moving" (*manneriae*). This transitional function establishes the *sequentia* as a category within the mass celebration. The *sequentia* completes a system of the four *modi* alternating between the historical, allegorical, analogical/ tropological, and eschatological modes, in combination, and in alternation with, the melodic *modi.*

schema: Greek term translated into Latin as *figura*: a delineating, linear outline that grants discretion, particularity, and individuality within inchoate mass (Plato, *Timaeus latinus,* Cassiodorus).

silva: Latin translation of Greek *hyle* (Chalcidius): literally a "forest full of trees," that is, *materia/substantia,* without limitation, boundaries, containment; without organization (*ordo*); without differentiation, congested and impacted mass (Quintilian); *substantia* (Cicero); *massa* (Augustine); a thicket; also a repository of preexistent substance available to be used for a specific purpose (Alfred the Great).

spatia: Space or interval of sound conceptualized as space, with high and low distinction (Martianus Capella).

spolia: Remains, ruins, primarily of Roman cities, buildings; an important concept of "what is there," that is, preexistent substance, to be used, appropriated, rearranged, for specific purposes. This concept of preexistent substance underlies a medieval conceptualization of the compositional process, in that one does not strive to be "original" but to use well what is already available.

symphonia: Consensus, "inner vigor" (Chalcidius).

theoria: Greek term for Latin *ductus/conductus*: a tri-partite model delineated and explained by Aristotle (*Metaphysics*) of a beginning, perplexing question (incipient moment) that then leads logically to a step-by-step process, one increment at a time, to a conclusion, or restful closure (cadence). This model is then exemplified in the *Physics* as directional motion that could be measured into infinitude, coming eventually to a point of rest, and is exemplified as the continuous process/motion of plot serving as a foundation, measured and differentiated by *figurae* in the *Poetics*. Even the *Secretum,* which apparently was not authored by Aristotle, illustrates this model in

terms of *currulum vitae.* Aristotle's *theoria* was perhaps most clearly understood through music exemplification, for example, by the *conductus (ductus,*
conduct).

tonus: Latin term for Greek *tonos:* particular, self-contained sound module,
separated from unlimited sound (*silva*), differentiated by delineatory *figura.*

tropus: Latin term for Greek *tropos:* most commonly used for analogy, metaphor (Quintilian), also indicative of the tropological *modus,* in which the
Latin *figura e* is prevalent as the concluding *figura,* indicating a command,
such as *psallite* ("Sing a psalm"), *laudate* ("Praise").

versus: "Enlivened body" (Augustine). The possibility is introduced that
the same principle of enclosed, contained "body" of enlivened substance
(Augustine's *pulsus*) can be extended or combined together into the
extended body of the *versus*—an additive, combinatory process rather than
one of difference (between *pulsus* and *versus*). *Versus* indicates an important
medieval concept that is not the same as, nor does it occur in a pair of opposites, as does "poetry" and "prose"—a much later distinction.

via recta: In the context of a discussion of *silva,* finding or making a way through
the disorganized, undifferentiated mass of possible *materia/substancia.* The
topos is an important one in the Middle Ages, both as an expression of this
duality between inchoate substance and individuation, as well as an articulation of mental, compositional work of any kind (Alfred the Great).

virga: Differentiating *figura* delineating characteristic features within unlimited substance. A "twig" separated out from the thicket of *silva,* and, as
such, a music notational *figura* that indicates, most typically, an accented
and/or higher tone.

vox: Enclosed, contained "body" of sound, important as illustrative of particularity, indicated by *figura,* that is, *virga, punctum.*

Selected Bibliography

PRIMARY SOURCES AND TRANSLATIONS

Alfred the Great

King Alfred's Old English Version of St. Augustine's Soliloquies, cf. Simon Keynes and Michael Lapidge, in *Alfred the Great. Asser's Life of King Alfred and Other Contemporary Sources* (Harmondsworth, UK/New York, 1983), pp. 138–139, based on the Anglo-Saxon edition of T. A. Carnicelli (Cambridge, MA, 1969), pp. 47–48.

Aristotle

Aristoteles latine interpretibus variis, ed. Academia Regia (Berlin, 1831; Nachdruck, Eckhard Kessler, Munich, 1995).
Aristoteles Latinus database.
The Complete Works of Aristotle, ed., trans. Jonathan Barnes, Bollingen Series 71.2, 2 vols. (Princeton, 1984).
Corpus latinum commentariorum in Aristotelem Graecorum, Opera (Turnhout, 1954–).

Augustine

Confessiones, ed., trans. Wilhelm Thimme (Düsseldorf, 2004).
De genesi ad litteram, PL XXXIV, CSEL XXVIII, ed. Josephus Zycha (Vienna/ Prague, 1894).
De musica, PL XXXII.
Sancti Aurelii Augustini, *Enarrationes in Psalmos,* in *Corpus Christianorum Series Latina* (Turnhout, 1956), pp. 38–40.

Boethius

Boetii, Manlii Severini, *Opera omnia,* in *Corpus Christianorum Series Latina* (Turnhout, 1957–); PL LXIV.
De arithmetica, ed. Henrici Oosthout, et al. (Turnhout, 1999).
De consolatione philosophiae, ed. Claudio Moreschini (Munich, 2005).

Cassiodorus

Expositio psalmorum, 2 vols., ed. Martin Adriaen, in *Corpus Christianorum Series Latina* (Turnhout, 1958).
Opera, in *Corpus Christianorum Series Latina* (Turnhout, 1958–1973).

Cicero

Concerning Invention (De inventione), ed., trans. H. M. Hubbell, Loeb Classical Library, Cicero Collected Works, vol. II (Cambridge, MA, 1949, repr. 1963).
The Nature of Gods (De natura deorum), ed., trans. H. Rackham, Loeb Classical Library, Cicero Collected Works, vol. 19 (Cambridge, MA, 1933, repr. 1994).

Dante Alighieri, *Inferno* from the *Divine Comedy, A Verse Translation* by Allen Mandelbaum with drawings by Barry Moser (Berkeley, Los Angeles, 1980; repr. 1982).
Johannes de Garlandia, *De mensurabili musica,* 2 vols., ed., comm.. Erich Reimer (Beihefte zum Archiv für Musikwissenschaft, 10–11; Wiesbaden, 1972).
De plana musica, ed., intro. Christian Meyer (Baden-Baden, 1998).

Johannes de Grocheio, *Die Quellenhandschriften zum Musiktraktat des Johannes de Grocheio,* ed., trans. Ernst Rohloff (Leipzig, 1972).

Grosseteste, Robert

Opera Roberti Grosseteste, ed. gen. James McEvoy, in *Corpus Christianorum Series Latina* (Turnhout, 1995–).
De cessatium legalium, ed. Richard C. Dales, Edward B. King, Auctores Britannici medii aevi, 7 (London, 1986).
De decem mandatis, ed. Richard C. Dales, Edward B. King, Auctores Britannici medii aevi, 10 (Oxford, 1987).
Hexaemeron, ed. Richard C. Dales, Servus Gieben, Auctores Britannici medii aevi, 6, Oxford (1982, repr. 1990).
Commentarius in posteriorum analyticorum libros, intro., comm. Pietro Rossi (Florence, 1981).
Works on Natural Science, *Die philosophischen Werke des Robert Grosseteste, Bischofs von Lincoln,* ed. Ludwig Baer (Munster i. W., 1912).

Guido of Arezzo, *Micrologus,* ed. Jos. Smits van Waesberghe, in *Corpus sciptorum de musica* (Rome, 1955).
Hugh of St. Victor, *Didascalicon,* ed., trans., intro. Jerome Taylor (New York, 1961; repr. 1991).
Isidore of Seville, *Etymologiae sive originum, libri XX.,* ed. W. M. Lindsay, Scriptorum classicorum bibliotheca Oxoniensis, 2 vols. (Oxford, 1985).
The Etymologies, trans., intro., notes Stephen A. Barney, et al., 3rd ed. (Cambridge, UK, 2007).
Liber usualis (Book for Use) (Tournai/New York, 1963).
Macrobius, *Commentary on the Dream of Scipio,* trans. William Harris Stahl (New York, 1952).
Martianus Capella and the Seven Liberal Arts, vol. 2, trans. William H. Stahl, Richard Johnson, E. L. Burge (New York, 1977).
Remigius of Auxerre, commentary on Martianus Capella, *Marriage of Philology and Mercury,* ed. Cora Lutz (Leiden, 1962).

Philip the Chancellor

Philippi Cancellarii Summa de bono ad fidem codicum primum edita studio et cura Nicolai Wicki, Opera philosophica mediae aetatis selecta, 2 vols. (Bern, 1985).

Plato

Phaedo, interprete Henrico Aristippo, ed. Laurentius Minio-Paluello, with H. J. Drossaart Lulofs, Corpus philosophorium medii aevi, Plato latinus, ed. gen. Raymond Klibansky (Leinden 1973).
Quintilian, *The Institutio Oratoria of Quintilian,* 4 vols., ed., trans. H. E. Butler, Loeb Classical Library (Cambridge, MA, 1920, repr. 1958).
Timaeus, *Collected Works IX,* trans. R. G. Bury, Loeb Classical Library (Cambridge, MA, 1929, repr. 1942, 1952, 1961, 1966, 1975, 1981).
Timaeus, a Calcidio translatus commentarioque instructus in societatem opera coniunto, ed. J. H. Waszink, Corpus philosophorum medii aevi, Plato latinus vol. 4, ed. gen. Raymond Klibansky (Leiden, 1962).

Virgil

The Aeneid, trans. Robert Fitzgerald (New York, 1990).
P. Vergili Maronis Opera, ed. R. A. B. Mynors (Oxford, 1969).

COLLECTED EDITIONS (WRITINGS ON MUSIC)

Corpus scriptorum de musica, American Institute of Musicology, Rome.
Scriptores ecclesiastici de musica sacra potissimum ex variis Italae, Galliae et Germaniae codibus manuscriptis collecti, ed. Martin Gerbert, 3 vols. (St. Blasian, 1784; repr. Berlin, 1905, Milan, 1931, Hildesheim, 1963).

Scriptorum de musica medii aevi, ed. Charles Edmond de Coussemaker, 4 vols. (Paris, 1864–1867, repr. Milan, 1931, Hildesheim, 1963).

REFERENCE WORKS AND COLLECTIONS

Analecta hymnica, ed. Guido Maria Dreves, et al., 55 vols. (Leipzig, 1886–1922).
Augustine, *Encyclopedia: Augustine through the Ages. An Encyclopedia,* ed. Allan D. Fitzgerald, O.S.A. (Grand Rapids, MI, 1999).
Cambridge History of Later Medieval Philosophy, ed. Norman Kretzman, et al. (Cambridge, UK, 1982).
Corpus Christianorum Series Latina.
Groves Dictionary of Music and Musicians, ed. Stanley Sadie (London, 1980).
Paléographie musicale.
Patrologiae latinae cursus completus . . . series *Latina,* ed. J-P Migne, 218 vols. (Paris, 1879–1890).

SECONDARY LITERATURE

Bately, Janet, "The Nature of Old English Prose," in *The Cambridge Companion to Old English Literature,* ed. Malcolm Godden and Michael Lapidge (Cambridge, UK, 1991).
Becker, A. L., *Beyond Translation* (Ann Arbor, MI, 1995).
Botticelli, Sandro, *Der Bilderzyklus zu Dantes Göttlicher Komodie,* ed. Hein-Th. Altcappenberg (London, 2000).
Brown, George H., "The Psalms as the Foundation of Anglo-Saxon Learning," in *The Place of the Psalms in the Intellectual Culture of the Middle Ages,* ed. Nancy van Deusen (Binghamton, NY, 1999), pp. 1–17.
Calvino, Italo, *The Castle of Crossed Destinies,* trans. William Weaver (New York, 1977).
Calvino, Italo, *If on a Winter's Day a Traveler,* trans. William Weaver (New York, 1979).
Calvino, Italo, *Italian Folk Tales,* selected and retold, trans. George Martin (San Diego, New York, London, 1980).
Carruthers, Mary, *The Craft of Thought. Meditation, Rhetoric, and the Making of Images, 400–1200* (Cambridge, UK, 1998).
Claussen, M. A., *The Reform of the Frankish Church. Chrodegang of Metz and the regula canonicorum in the Eighth Century* (Cambridge, UK, 2004).
Contreni, John J., *Codex Laudunensis 468. A Ninth Century Guide to Virgil, Sedulius, and the Liberal Arts,* Armarium Codicum Insignium, vol. 3 (Turnhout, 1984).
Dod, Bernard G., "Aristoteles latinus," in *Cambridge History of Later Medieval Philosophy,* ed. Norman Kretzman, et al. (Cambridge, UK, 1982), pp. 45–79.
Dronke, Peter, *The Spell of Calcidius. Platonic Concepts and Images in the Medieval West* (Florence, 2008).

Dyer, Joseph, "The Psalms in Monastic Prayer," in *The Place of the Psalms in the Intellectual Culture of the Middle Ages*, ed. Nancy van Deusen (Binghamton, NY, 1999), pp. 53–83.

Flynn, William T., *Medieval Music as Medieval Exegesis* (Lanham, MD, 1999).

Gauer, Werner, "Konstantin und die Geschichte. Zu den 'Spolien' am Konstantinsbogen und zur Schlangensäule," in *Panchaia. Festschrift für Klaus Thraede. Jahrbuch für Antike und Christentum*, Ergänzungsband 22 (Münster, 1995), pp. 131–140.

Gersh, Stephen, *Concord in Discourse: Harmonics and Semiotics in Late Classical and Early Medieval Platonism* (Berlin, 1996).

Glorieux, Palémon, *Répertoire des Maîtres en théologie de Paris au XIIIe siècle*, 2 vols. (Paris, 1933–1934).

Green, Peter, *Classical Bearings: Interpreting Ancient History and Culture* (Berkeley, Los Angeles, 1989).

Green-Pedersen, Niels J. *The Tradition of the Topics in the Middle Ages* (Munich, 1984).

Grout, Donald J., *A History of Western Music* (New York, 1960).

Hübner, Wolfgang, "Der ordo der Realien in Augustins Frühdialog *De ordine*," *Revue des Etudes Augustiniennes* 33 (1987), 23–48.

Humbert, J. "A propos de Ciceron traducteur de grec," *Mélanges de Phil., de Litt., et d'Hist. Anc. offerts d. A. Ernout* (1940), 197–200.

Kaczynski, Bernice, "Translations: Latin and Greek," in *Medieval Latin: An Introduction and Bibliographical Guide*, ed. F.A.C. Mantello, A.G. Rigg (Washington DC, 1996), pp. 718–722.

Klibansky, Raymond, *The Continuity of the Platonic Tradition: Plato's Parmenides in the Middle Ages* (London, 1939, repr. 1982, 1984).

Kuczynski, Michael P., "The Psalms and Social Action in Late Medieval England," in *The Place of the Psalms in the Intellectual Culture of the Middle Ages*, ed. Nancy van Deusen (Binghamton, NY, 1999), pp. 173–195.

Lapidge, Michael, "Surviving Booklists from Anglo-Saxon England," in *Learning and Literature in Anglo-Saxon England. Studies Presented to Peter Clemoes on the Occasion of his Sixty-Fifth Birthday*, ed. Michael Lapidge, and Helmut Gneuss (Cambridge, UK, 1985).

de Lubac, Henri, *Exégèse médiévale. Les quatre sens de l'écriture* (Paris, 1959).

MacCormack, Sabine, *The Shadows of Poetry: Vergil in the Mind of Augustine* (Berkeley-Los Angeles, 1998).

Marenbon, John, "Medieval Latin Commentaries and Glosses on Aristotelian Logical Texts before c. 1150 A.D.," in *Aristotelian Logic, Platonism, and the Context of Early Medieval Philosophy in the West* (London, 2000), pp. 77–127; 128–140.

Mathiesen, Thomas J., *Apollo's Lyre. Greek Music and Music Theory in Antiquity and the Middle Ages* (Lincoln, NE, 1999).

McCormick, Michael, *Five Hundred Unknown Glosses from the Palatine Virgil*, The Vatican Library Ms Pal. Lat 1631 (Studi e Testi 343, Vatican, 1992).

McKirahan, Jr., Richard D., *Philosophy Before Socrates. An Introduction with Texts and Commentary* (Indianapolis/Cambridge, 1994).

Mitchell, Melanie, *Complexity. A Guided Tour* (Oxford, 2009).

Reese, Gustave, *Music in the Middle Ages* (New York, 1940).

Schroer, Klaus, and Klaus Irle, ". . . *Ich aber quadrere den Kreis . . .* " *Leonardo da Vincis Proportionsstudie* (Münster, 1998).

Seebass, Tilman, *Musikdarstellung und Psalterillustration im früheren Mittelalter*, 2 vols. (Bern, Switzerland, 1973).

Smalley, Beryl, *The Study of the Bible in the Middle Ages* (repr. Notre Dame, Indiana, 1964; third printing, 1978).

Stock, Brian, *Myth and Science in the Twelfth Century: A Study of Bernard Silvester* (Princeton, 1972).

Stump, Eleanor, "Dialectic," in *The Seven Liberal Arts in the Middle Ages*, ed. David L. Wagner (Bloomington, IN, 1986), pp. 125–146.

Stump, Eleanor, "Garlandus Compotista and Dialectic in the Eleventh and Twelfth Centuries," *History and Philosophy of Logic* I (1980), 1–18.

van Deusen, Nancy, "Roger Bacon on Music," in *Roger Bacon and the Sciences*, ed. Jeremiah Hackett (Leiden, 1997), pp. 223–241.

van Deusen, Nancy, "The *figura* of Fauvel: Modality Applied in the Roman de Fauvel," in *The Harp and the Soul: Essays in Medieval Music* (Lewiston, New York, 1989), pp. 329–383.

van Deusen, Nancy, *Music at Nevers Cathedral: Principal Sources of Medieval Chant*, 2 vols. (Binningen, Switzerland, 1980).

van Deusen, Nancy, "*de Musica, De Ordine*," in *Augustine through the Ages: An Encyclopedia*, ed. Allan D. Fitzgerald, O.S.A. (Grand Rapids, MI, 1999).

van Deusen, Nancy, "Origins of a Significant Medieval Genre: The Musical 'Trope' to the Twelfth Century," *Rhetorica (Journal of the History of Rhetoric)* 3 (1985), 245–267.

van Deusen, Nancy, "The Problem of Matter, the Nature of Mode, and the Example of Melody in Medieval Music Writing," in *The Harp and the Soul: Essays in Medieval Music* (Lewiston, New York, 1989), pp. 1–45.

van Deusen, Nancy, *Theology and Music at the Early University: The Case of Robert Grosseteste and Anonymous IV* (Leiden, 1995).

van Deusen, Nancy, "The Use and Significance of the Sequence," *Musica Disciplina* 40 (1986), 1–46.

van Deusen, Nancy, "On the Usefulness of Music: Motion, Music, and the Thirteenth-Century Reception of Aristotle's *Physics*," *Viator* 29 (1998), 167–187.

van Winden, J.C.M. *Calcidius on Matter, His Doctrine and Sources* (Leiden, 1959).

Weber, Eugen, "What Is Real in Folk Tales," in *My France: Politics, Culture, Myth* (Cambridge, MA, 1991).

Whittow, Mark, *The Making of Byzantium 600–1025* (Cambridge, UK, 1996).

Wilson, Adrian, and Joyce Lancaster Wilson, *A Medieval Mirror. Speculum humanae salvationis, 1324–1500* (Berkeley / Los Angeles, 1984).

Index

About the Author

NANCY VAN DEUSEN holds a PhD in musicology from Indiana University, Bloomington; is currently professor of musicology and Benezet Professor of the Humanities at Claremont Graduate University; and is director of the Claremont Consortium in Medieval and Early Modern Studies, Claremont Colleges and Graduate University. She has taught at Indiana University; the University of Basel, Switzerland; the University of North Carolina, Chapel Hill; Central European University, Budapest; and within the California State University system. She has received American Philosophical Society, NEH, and Fulbright grants; and she has published on music within the medieval city of Rome, music, liturgy, and institutional structure within the medieval cathedral milieu of Nevers, France, the medieval sequence within its Latin codicological and paleographical contexts, as well as its significance for the history of ideas; and music as medieval science and within the curriculum of the early university.